A CRY FROM THE STREETS

Rescuing Brazil's Forgotten Children

JEANNETTE LUKASSE

YWAM Publishing is the publishing ministry of Youth With A Mission. Youth With A Mission (YWAM) is an international missionary organization of Christians from many denominations dedicated to presenting Jesus Christ to this generation. To this end, YWAM has focused its efforts in three main areas: 1) training and equipping believers for their part in fulfilling the Great Commission (Matthew 28:19); 2) personal evangelism; 3) mercy ministry (medical and relief work).

For a free catalog of books and materials write or call:
YWAM Publishing
P.O. Box 55787, Seattle, WA 98155
(425) 771-1153 or (800) 922-2143
www.ywampublishing.com

A Cry from the Streets: Rescuing Brazil's Forgotten Children

Copyright © 2002 by YWAM Publishing

10 09 08 07 06 05 04 03 02   10 9 8 7 6 5 4 3 2 1

Published by Youth With A Mission Publishing
P.O. Box 55787
Seattle, WA 98155

Originally published in the Dutch language under the title *God's Hart Voor Kinderen* by Uitgeverij Gideon, Hoornaar, Holland, © 2000 by Uitgeverij Gideon. All rights reserved.

Translated from Dutch by Aubrey Beauchamp.

Some Scripture quotations in this book are taken from the Holy Bible, New International Version®, Copyright© 1973, 1978, 1984 by the International Bible Society. Used by permission of Zondervan Publishing House. Others are taken from the New King James Version, Copyright © 1979, 1980, 1982 by Thomas Nelson, Inc., Publishers. Used by permission.

ISBN 1-57658-263-9

Printed in the United States of America.

Other International Adventures

Contents

Foreword

by Chuck Smith Jr.

D O E S it take exceptional people to create a vibrant mission to suffering children, or does steadfast commitment to missions create exceptional people? Perhaps you will find an answer to this question in the warm and engaging story of an average couple who followed the leading of God one step at a time—from the Netherlands to Belo Horizonte, Brazil.

Few English-speaking people are aware of the condition of the "disposable children" in South America. Children, as young as five or six, end up living on the streets for many different reasons. Some of them are true orphans. Others have fled homes where they received daily, merciless beatings. Others have been thrown out of their homes because a new father moved in who doesn't want them or another baby was added to the already overcrowded apartment and there was no more room for them.

The street children are literally on their own. If they will eat, they must find food. If they sleep, they must find a safe place and some way to stay warm and dry. Forget birthday parties, new shoes, or education. Their challenge is to stay alive.

The riveting first chapter of this book will give you a brief encounter with the street kids of Belo Horizonte. As the story unfolds, you will discover the heartbreaking misery that is their lives. But you will also learn about God's magnificent love for them and how He has gradually provided them a refuge, a family, an education, healing, and hope.

Read this book and learn of the extraordinary things God has done for the "least of His brothers" through a handful of people who have surrendered to His guidance. We need to know about the crimes against children that are both outrageous and preventable. But we also need to know that these children are not forgotten by God.

Jeannette's smooth and autobiographical style makes this not only an easy book to read, but also one that is pleasant and entertaining. My guess is that by the fourth or fifth chapter you will begin to realize the extraordinary things God can do with your life, and that you will begin praying some of the same prayers that Johan and Jeannette have prayed. I pray that it will please God to increase the faith and compassion of everyone who comes across this wonderful story.

Chuck Smith Jr. is the senior pastor of Calvary Chapel in Capistrano Beach, California.

Foreword

by Brother Andrew

T H E Old Testament closes with the Lord's statement that the prophet Elijah "will turn the hearts of the fathers to their children, and the hearts of the children to their fathers; or else I will come and strike the land with a curse" (Malachi 4:6). After some four hundred years of silence in Scripture, an angel of the Lord prophesied that John the Baptist "will go on before the Lord, in the spirit and power of Elijah, to turn the hearts of the fathers to their children and the disobedient to the wisdom of the righteous—to make ready a people prepared for the Lord" (Luke 1:17).

Clearly, the position of the hearts of fathers and children toward each other is an indication of a people's spiritual condition and is greatly important to God. The heart of God is always turned toward His children, drawing us to turn toward Him. Sadly it is not always so with fathers and mothers on earth.

Children do not have it within their power to be the first to turn— to turn to their "fathers," to change, to seek protection, education, love, and care, or above all to be taught in the ways of Jesus. The fathers have to change first. How can children make responsible decisions in a society where people seek only their own interests and exploit every- thing and everyone around them? Children don't have the resources that adults have. They are stuck between a rock and a hard place—a very hard place. The tragic result is that millions of children, especially in Latin America, are rejected and abandoned. Yet all the time God is looking for fathers—real fathers for these throw-away street kids.

To many of these children, the Lukasse family has become just that: the fathers they need. I happen to know this family, because they are members of my home church in the Netherlands. We meet occasionally when they are on furlough, and two of my own children and their spouses have volunteered with their ministry in Brazil. In a small way, our church supports them and prays for them.

I trust that everyone who reads this compelling book will share the burden for the multitudes of unreached children for whom God is still looking for fathers. No, I must not preach; this book is powerful enough.

What a tremendous gift God has imparted to Jeannette to write so eloquently, warmly, and compassionately about the problems that are all around us—problems with families, individuals, and above all, problems with children. Most of us would like to pretend that these problems do not exist, or we'd like to convince ourselves that if they do exist, there is nothing we can do. But there are things we can do.

That faraway country with its *favelas* (slums) and its millions of street children is no farther away from God's heart than the kids He gave us: our own children. So why not embrace them as the Lukasses did? Why not allow God to break our hearts as He did theirs?

Brother Andrew is the author of God's Smuggler *and the founder of Open Doors, an international ministry to the worldwide suffering church. He lives in the Netherlands.*

Police Brutality

S U D D E N L Y a group of angry police officers surrounded our ministry team on a downtown sidewalk. The ragtag street children who were huddled around the team jumped up and bolted. Two of the smaller ones weren't quite fast enough. A skinny officer, his bony face contorted with rage, grabbed them both by the scruffs of their necks and, yelling obscenities, hit their little heads with a thud against a concrete wall. The children collapsed on the littered pavement. Now the police officer really lost control and moved in on Mati, one of our team members.

It was eleven o'clock Friday night in Belo Horizonte, a large city in Brazil. As was their practice, a few members of our staff had gone to the downtown area. They knew the children's favorite hangouts, and soon twenty-five or so hungry, grimy street children were gathered around them. The team doled out sandwiches and chocolate milk to the children and bandaged some of their open wounds. Then they all sat down on the pavement in small groups and played board games and checkers.

Julio, the team leader that evening, strummed his guitar and patiently explained some basic chords to a little boy. With his long, slender fingers, he created beautiful music. Fascinated, the little guy watched him and then, with great concentration, tried to bend his dirty, stubby fingers over the guitar strings.

In spite of the late hour, the large red-and-blue city buses were still crowded. Each time a bus rumbled past, the little group was enveloped in putrid exhaust fumes. Typical South American samba music blared from the many rundown bars. Bright neon signs pulsated through the stifling night air, inviting customers to the drab tables and folding chairs on the narrow sidewalk. The legion of children who live here are used to this chaos of odors and sounds and colors. After all, this is their home. They play, eat, and sleep on the streets.

Julio scanned the motley group around him. His charges were quiet tonight, he observed, obviously enjoying the games and the attention. That quietness was rudely shattered, however, with the arrival of the incensed law officers.

One tall, angry police officer zeroed in on Mati, a young, muscular Samoan. Two other officers wildly kicked and hit anyone within reach. Quickly Julio jumped up but could not avoid several blows before he reached Mati.

"Stop!" he yelled. "We're missio—"

Wham! A well-aimed punch hit Julio right in the face. The frenzied police officers seemed determined to beat everyone to a pulp. More patrol cars, sirens shrieking, pulled up. Dodging blows, Julio and his team tried to explain that they were missionaries and hadn't done anything wrong, but the enraged law officers appeared to be completely out of control and in no mood to listen to anyone.

Mati was strong enough to overpower the officers, but he didn't even try. Confused, he just raised his arms to shield his head from the barrage of blows aimed at his face. He was not a fighter. It fact, it was Mati's nonviolent nature that had endeared him to his coworkers. The furious officers didn't let up, but continued to kick and punch Mati and anyone else within their reach. At the height of the aggression, a few officers grabbed Mati, squeezed him into the back of a large, gray police vehicle, and screeched off into the night. The other patrol cars, sirens still blaring, followed, leaving behind a cloud of dust and a stunned team.

Some team members were crying, not because of the beating but because of their mounting fear of what was likely to happen to Mati. They knew that Mati's life was in grave danger. After all, this was normal police behavior toward most of the six million unwanted street children in this vast country. Our ministry staff was all too familiar with the gruesome stories of police brutality—children being rounded up and transported to dark, deserted areas outside the city to be tortured and killed. Mati, with his dark skin, could easily pass for a Brazilian. Had the police mistaken him for a gang leader?

Lately the Brazilian police had been rather frustrated. The government had just passed a law, compliments of Protective Child Care Services, that, among other things, made it illegal to transport street children in the trunk of a police car or to beat them up at precincts. The officers felt that this law had pulled the rug out from under their authority on the streets. In protest, they ignored the children altogether. Not surprisingly, it didn't take the street-smart youngsters long to take advantage of this situation. Some children had even memorized the code number of this new law, yelling it out to taunt passing police in their patrol cars.

In addition, some unscrupulous barbers were offering street children up to two dollars for a pound of human hair for making wigs. As a result, girls with beautiful, long hair were suddenly surrounded by gangs of street children and roughly pulled into an alley. There, held down by strong arms, they would be relieved of their long locks. This wasn't a compassionate procedure. The thieves used anything that would cut: dull scissors, kitchen knives, switchblades, and even daggers. When these practices were reported, the police did nothing. Citizens became enraged. Newspaper headlines condemned the young thugs. Petrified women, scarves tightly wrapped around their heads, scurried along the crowded downtown streets. Still nothing had been done, and tension was mounting.

Apparently the police weren't ignoring the children anymore—at least not on this night.

I HAD just fallen asleep. My husband, Johan, was attending a two-week YWAM (Youth With A Mission) conference in Budapest, so I had our double bed all to myself. Our five children had been in bed for hours. Carla, one of our coworkers who had moved in while Johan was gone, had also retired for the night. Suddenly someone pounded on my bedroom door.

"Jeannette, come quickly! Mati has been arrested!"

Half-awake, I stumbled out of bed and opened the door. There stood a panic-stricken Carla.

"Jeannette, please hurry. Sofia just came back from downtown and said the police arrested Mati!"

"What?!" I spotted Sofia in the kitchen sobbing. "What happened?" I asked, now wide-awake.

"The cops beat us up and took Mati," Sofia cried.

Sofia, a small, levelheaded Dutch woman, was not easily provoked. That night she had left her husband in charge of their four children to join the street team. They were both dedicated workers and had been with us for several years.

"What about Julio? Where is he?" I asked.

Helplessly Sofia shook her head and said, "He told me to take the team home while he followed Mati."

I quickly got dressed. "Sofia, wake up everyone right away and have them start praying! I'll make some calls and see if anyone can help."

Our staff of forty, plus twenty-five ex-street boys, lived in a large building we called Restoration House. Even though it was well after midnight, in no time I could hear many voices praying in the dining room.

I decided to call a friend from church, a Brazilian lieutenant colonel with the military police. As I dialed the number, I felt grateful to have friends we could call in the middle of the night. An hour and a half later, which seemed like an eternity, my friend found out through his police-car radio that Mati was being held prisoner in an empty room at the central bus station. Immediately three of our staff and I drove to the station. It was now 2 A.M., more than two hours since Mati's arrest.

The police had taken Mati to the empty central bus station right away to torture him. In that empty room the police forced him to face a concrete wall, and then ten of the police officers kicked him in the crotch until he fainted. When he regained consciousness, the police beat him some more until he collapsed again.

Our arrival at the bus station surprised the officers. Some tried to stall us while others hastily hustled Mati back into the patrol car and tore off. In the nick of time we spotted them and, with tires screeching, gave chase. It turned into a wild pursuit from broad, well-lit streets to narrow, dark alleys. With my heart pounding, we raced against traffic on major one-way streets. The chase finally ended in a narrow, poorly lit street in front of a dark police station. The police roughly pulled Mati from the car and pushed him quickly through the grimy door into a small, dingy room, where he promptly collapsed. I bolted from our car, pushed my way through the door, found Mati, and knelt beside him. Slowly he sat up and opened his swollen, bloodshot eyes. When he recognized me, he began to cry.

During this long, hot pursuit I had felt very angry with these police officers—angry that they had arrested Mati in the first place and angry that they had then tortured him without even asking who he was or what he was doing. I was convinced we could take Mati home once these crazed men realized who we were. I was wrong. Before I could say a word, one of the officers tried to jerk me away from Mati, but he grabbed my hand and wouldn't let go. The police officer kicked Mati's hand and cursed me. Mati moaned, let go, and again fell to the floor.

Now I was really boiling mad, but before I could utter a sound, I was shoved into a small, stuffy room. With a smirk, the police officer walked over to an old television set and cranked up the volume full blast. Then he stomped out of the room and slammed the door behind him. It was obvious no one was interested in explanations. I was worried sick. Mati had a heart condition. Just a year ago we had had to rush him twice to the emergency room with an irregular heart rhythm. I wasn't sure what those wild policemen had done to him, but I could tell he was in great pain.

Here I was, a mother of five, held hostage in the middle of the night in an obscure police station in the heart of Brazil.

Lord! my heart screamed. *You called us to this country. Please, do something!*

Turning Points

A S   F A R   back as I can remember, I knew that God loved me and that I was His child. As a four-year-old walking the few blocks to preschool, I would often take a detour to the local dump. I would climb onto that big mountain of trash, sit down, and talk to God. I had learned a song: "In valleys and on mountains, yes, God is everywhere!" Since there are neither mountains nor valleys in my flat, native country of the Netherlands, the only mountain I could find was the trash heap.

My parents encouraged my six-year-older sister, Carla, and me to attend Sunday school at a local church in the center of our "cheese city" of Gouda. I don't recall ever hearing anything about missions, but when I was six years old I announced, "When I grow up I'm going to Brazil to start an orphanage." I further explained that those orphans would get plenty to eat and, most important to me at the time, lots of candy and cookies.

When I was thirteen, a friend took me to a Bible study led by a police officer and his wife. Every Wednesday evening about forty young people crammed into the couple's living room to study the Bible. Among this group of mostly high school and college students were a few former drug addicts the officer had met after their arrests. The officer had shared the love of God with these young men and invited them to the Bible study. Since some of these young men had been notorious drug traffickers, I was very impressed to observe firsthand the tremendous changes God had wrought in their lives.

Another regular at the Bible study was a tall, bright young man. What struck me about him was his enthusiasm during worship. Sitting cross-legged on the floor, his upper body gently swayed with the rhythms of the music while his eyes, under a head of unruly brown hair, shone like stars. His name was Johan, and he was studying at Driestar College for his teaching credential. Johan was from the province of Zeeland and came from a family of eleven children. His parents were deeply religious, and every Sunday the family filled several pews in the little Reformed church in their village of Hoedekenskerke.

When Johan grew up, he became disillusioned with God and the church. They failed to hold his attention, and he couldn't understand why his family called God a God of love. If God really existed, he reasoned, why did He allow people to make such a mess of the world? At age sixteen, when he began his studies at Driestar, he was glad he could move into the student quarters and get away from home. Freedom beckoned. Even though this was a Christian college with strict rules, he figured he wouldn't be reminded of God here as often as he would be at home. Perhaps he could also get rid of the morbid fear of God with which he had been raised.

Then one day one of his roommates had asked, "Say, Johan, do you think God speaks to us? I mean, does He really personally know us?"

Surprised, Johan looked up. "What are you talking about?"

"Well," his roommate shrugged, a little too nonchalantly, "a couple of days ago my mother gave me this book she picked up at a Bible study. I just finished reading it."

The young man seemed a little uncomfortable. Johan waited.

"Well, eh…," the roommate continued, "if the story in this book is true and God actually speaks to us and loves each of us personally, then…eh…then *we* can also hear and understand *His* voice."

An awkward silence followed.

Incredulous, Johan stared at the young man in front of him. "What book are you talking about?" he finally asked.

His friend handed him a small paperback titled *The Cross and the Switchblade.* Johan didn't quite know what to think.

"May I read it?" he proposed. "At the end of the week I'll let you know what I think."

Relieved, his friend nodded and walked off.

That same day Johan began to read. The story was about a young pastor from the Midwest, David Wilkerson, whom God told to go to New York City to tell notorious gang members that He loves them. The author explained in detail how God had led him step-by-step toward this daunting goal. The story both fascinated and irritated Johan.

"Either this David is a liar," he finally reported back to his friend, "or God is completely different from what I have always believed Him to be."

Johan had decided to go to the Bible study and find out for himself. It hadn't taken him long to realize that God indeed loved him and that Jesus, God's Son, had died for his, Johan's, sins. Johan finally understood that God the Father, as proof of His love for the world, had offered the life of His Son. God wasn't far from His people after all. He wasn't angry either but loved them deeply.

In the meantime I was having my own watershed experience with God. I was now sixteen and had decided to tell God exactly what I wanted from Him. I had two requests, written out like some sort of contract. First of all, I wanted a boyfriend. The thought of remaining single all my life didn't appeal to me. Second, I had changed my mind about being a missionary, which I had proclaimed to the world since I was six. I decided I liked living in the Netherlands, and besides, being a missionary could be dangerous. For three weeks I faithfully presented God with these two items every night as I knelt by my bed.

Lord, if You do these two things for me, I prayed, *I will follow You the rest of my life.*

Strangely enough, every day I grew less satisfied with these petitions and sensed deep in my heart that God wasn't pleased with them either. Night after night I attempted to convince God it really was a good deal, but it seemed my prayers kept falling on deaf ears. Finally, while kneeling at my bed one night, I became so miserable I burst into tears.

"Okay, Lord," I sobbed, "I can't stand Your silence anymore. Please show me what I am doing wrong."

To my utter surprise, God immediately answered my request. He spoke to my heart as clearly as though He had spoken in an audible voice.

Jeannette, He said, *I want* all *of your life, one hundred percent, with no restrictions. If I want you to be a missionary or to marry or to do something quite different—that's My decision, not yours. I want you to leave everything to Me. Just trust Me.*

Instantly, I realized I had no business telling God what to do. I belonged to Him, and He could do with my life whatever He wanted. However, in spite of that knowledge, I still found it difficult to totally commit my life to Him. I knew God had given me a free will, and if I wanted to stay in control and make my own decisions, He would let me.

That night, after a struggle that lasted several hours, I was finally able to be totally honest with God and give Him permission to do whatever He wanted with my life. Instantly, the heavy load fell from my shoulders. Suddenly I was willing to go into missions, and though it may sound strange for a sixteen-year-old, I was even willing not to marry, if that's what God had in mind for me. Little did I realize at the time that Mr. Bright Eyes from our Bible study and I would one day be going steady.

The following year our Bible study group attended a large conference in England. While there, Johan and I had an opportunity to spend some time together and get to know each other better. After a few weeks we were madly in love and convinced that God had brought us together. I was floating on cloud nine.

One of our favorite hangouts was Gouda's market square in front of the famous sixteenth-century gothic city hall. We often sat on the worn steps leading to the massive front doors, savoring ice cream cones from the Italian soda fountain.

"Do you think God wants to do something about the suffering and pain in the world?" Johan asked me one day while licking his dripping cone.

"Sure," I answered, gazing at the bustling square. "I think God is very concerned."

"But do you think God wants *us* to do something about it?" Johan insisted. "You know, if God wants to help those who suffer, He usually does it by using people, don't you think?"

Surprised, I prodded, "Are you saying you think God may use *us* to help other people?"

"Yes, I am. I would really like for God to use us in such a way that our lives will make a big difference in the world." He sounded serious.

"Don't you think that's kind of arrogant?" I asked.

Johan shifted his weight. "No, not really. Why do we have so much and other people in poor countries, so little? Look at the things we have been given: good health, plenty of food, an excellent education. I believe we have been given these things so that we can pass some of them along to others."

The city hall chimes rang out their familiar tune. Silently we pondered these possibilities. We hadn't quite yet grasped the concept that God had explained to Abraham way back in the Old Testament that Abraham had been blessed so that he in turn could bless others. However, we were now beginning to consider this idea, and God would continue to reveal His plan for our lives.

THREE

Does God Really Want Us?

AFTER graduating from high school, I wanted to get involved in health care and applied for nurse's training. I was accepted at Refaja Hospital in Dordrecht and moved to the student quarters. Here, for the first time in my life, I was directly confronted with suffering and death. Deeply moved, I shed many tears, especially on the pediatrics floor.

During that time Johan earned his teaching credential. He was offered a job in Zuidland, a small village about an hour's drive from Dordrecht. Riding his old BMW motorcycle, he came to visit me as often as he could. He enjoyed his new job and constantly came up with new, creative ideas for his students: innovative games, sporting events, or special craft projects. Soon he was one of the most popular teachers.

After going steady for three years, we were married and were fortunate to find a nice three-room apartment in Dordrecht. After a wonderful wedding attended by many friends and relatives and Johan's entire class, we spent our honeymoon in Tunisia. My happiness was complete.

Our quarters in Dordrecht were tiny and very cozy. Johan had built all our furniture, including our big four-poster bed, which barely fit into our bedroom. Since I often managed to get the same days off as Johan, we were able to spend a lot of time together. I was in my second year of nurse's training, and even though my mother often hinted that our home was less than orderly, I thought it no big deal to combine my studies with running a household. Sure, at times Johan's socks emerged slightly pink from our secondhand washing machine, and often the dishes piled up for a week, but we didn't care.

Eighteen months later I graduated from nursing school and was offered a job as a staff nurse. Suddenly classes and study didn't tie me down anymore. I was even free to leave my job and do something else. Possibilities abounded. We had often daydreamed about a variety of options for our future. Like most Dutch people, we had lived frugally; we had even saved enough to live on for a while without an income.

The most logical thing to do was to keep our jobs and buy a home. We could use the space, and a house would be a good investment. A second option was more adventurous: a trip around the world on our shiny black tandem bike. Many an evening we pored over various world maps to figure out how many countries we could explore. A third possibility was based more on an inner feeling of unrest, an urge to do something useful with our lives, to not just live for our own pleasure but to be used by God in a place where help was needed. The question was, Did God want us, and if so, where?

We decided to pray about it during a week's vacation while canoeing along Holland's many waterways. We packed a pup tent, sleeping bags, powdered milk, cereal, and peanuts and stashed it all at the front of the canoe, and off we went. Spring had just arrived, but the weather was still chilly, especially in the morning. We rowed leisurely along endless miles of narrow, scenic rivers. Fat black-and-white Friesian cows, gorging themselves on a lush supply of tall grass, looked up in unhurried surprise as we glided along the dew-drenched banks. At home, our lives had clipped along at a brisk pace, and this rural, peaceful environment quieted our spirits. Every day we earnestly studied the Word and prayed.

Someone had told us about a small mission base in the north of Holland that was run by a new organization called Youth With A Mission, or YWAM for short. It didn't offer the standard four-year training, as did many mission organizations. Instead, YWAM's training course, called Discipleship Training School, or DTS, lasted only nine months, three of which were to be spent abroad participating in an evangelism outreach. The entire training was geared toward students getting more intimately acquainted with God and then sharing this knowledge with others. What really appealed to us about this type of training was the practical part.

Cozy and warm, we were relaxing one evening in our sleeping bags in our little pup tent. The canoe was moored along the bank. Johan, hands folded behind his head, mused, "I believe if we take a course like that we'll find out whether or not we're supposed to be in missions."

"That means we have to quit our jobs and let go of our apartment," I reminded him. "That's kind of drastic, isn't it?"

Johan turned over, gently put his hand on my slightly distended belly, and nodded. "And what about the baby?" he said softly. "You're right, pretty soon it won't be just you and me any longer. Would this really be a responsible decision?" Deep in thought, he frowned.

"However, if we don't do it now, we never will," he continued. "Can you imagine our frustration once we are happily settled in our new home, watching all the suffering in the world and knowing that we never even *tried* to find out if we were supposed to do anything about it?" Johan sat up to emphasize his words.

"Jeannette," he proposed, leaning back on one elbow, "let's give it a year. Let's give the Lord a chance to call us before we settle down and get into a rut. After all, we prayed about it this whole week. I really feel that's what we're supposed to do. What do you say?"

Tenderly he stroked my hair and waited for my response.

"Well," I admitted, "I have more peace about it than buying a home or taking a trip around the world."

Relieved, he smiled and hugged me. Suddenly my doubts about the future evaporated. Here I was with my wonderful husband, exploring the kind of plans God might have for us.

"Okay," I whispered. "Maybe we are nuts, but let's do it."

" Y O U want to do what! Are you crazy?" the doctor on my floor hollered when he heard our plans. "Where in the world did you get such a dumb idea?"

Disgusted, he turned to my supervisor and, pointing a finger at me, blurted, "Do you know what Jeannette wants to do? Save the blind heathens!" Incredulous, he stomped off.

The supervisor gave me a quizzical look. "What's he talking about?"

I was still reeling from his stinging criticism.

"He asked about my plans for the future," I said in a daze, "and I told him we're going to take a course to find out about missions."

She gave me a blank look and said, "Oh."

Okay, I thought, *so not everyone is excited about our plans.* Actually, with the exception of our Bible study friends, everyone else we knew also disapproved. With a baby on the way, they felt it was an irresponsible decision. Even our own immediate families secretly hoped it was a passing fancy. Yet every day we became more convinced we had made the right decision, because God was giving us, in spite of our many uncertainties, a deep peace.

The Call

W I T H a final jerk, Johan pulled the rope taut across our loaded trailer. Today was moving day, and we were very excited. The backseat of our small orange sports car was crammed to the hilt. Even in front—on the floor and on my lap—we had stuffed many items I thought might come in handy in our new home. Now seven months pregnant, I barely fit in the front seat and, once in place with a lap full of boxes, didn't think I would ever be able to get out. Because of my convictions, I had been fairly successful in squelching recurring doubts about this venture. Now, uncomfortably wedged among our belongings, I felt those doubts resurface.

We had been informed we would have only one room at the YWAM base, which was called Heidebeek. Johan had made us a sofa bed, since taking our large four-poster was out of the question. We also needed space for a crib. A small antique desk would double as a diaper-changing station. During my last three months at work, while on night duty, I had crocheted little blue curtains and sewed a blue quilt for the bed. With those and our off-yellow rugs, I planned to transform our room into a cozy little abode.

The drive to the base took much longer than planned, as our cargo slowed us down considerably. Early in the afternoon we finally arrived in the city of Heerde. In the wooded outskirts we found our destination: a large, thatched-roof house, idyllically located among towering trees. Dark-blue shutters contrasted sharply with the whitewashed walls. We turned slowly into the driveway and parked. From behind the building a young woman approached us. When she spotted our little caravan she stopped dead in her tracks and slapped her hand across her mouth.

"How many people is all this for?" she asked.

Johan glanced at me. "Just for us," he explained. "My wife, our baby, and me."

I felt awkward and embarrassed. Why in the world had we brought all this stuff anyway? At the gate I noticed another young man arriving. He carried one solitary suitcase.

Meanwhile, the young woman was still eyeing our car and trailer.

"I'll show you your room," she said, finding her voice again. "I hope you'll be able to get everything in."

Johan extricated me from the car. Our enthusiasm was evaporating. Suddenly becoming aware of the biting wind, I shivered. The sun hid behind an ominous gray cloud. Silently we unloaded the car and trailer and piled everything in front of the big house. My doubts were sprouting like mushrooms.

Lord, I prayed silently, *would You please help us feel at home here?*

The baby inside me kicked.

And Lord, I added, *please take care of our baby.*

All my insecurities were back in full force. Tears stung my eyes. I swallowed hard and sternly reminded myself that this had been our own decision. Hadn't we come here to offer our lives to God? With a deep sigh I picked up a bag. *Okay, Lord, here we are!*

FIFTY-FIVE students from Holland, the United States, and England had signed up for the DTS course. That first day it took a while for all of us to locate our rooms and settle in. We actually managed to get all our furniture into our room, even though it was a snug fit. The blue curtains went up, and after a good night's rest, we felt much more at ease. A kind neighbor even loaned us a wicker bassinet from his attic that found a place of honor on our small table in the corner of our room.

Classes were held every morning and evening, and each week we had a different teacher. Many had been involved for many years with Youth With A Mission or other mission organizations. They came with rich treasures of personal experience, and like sponges, we soaked it all up. One particular evening in October left a deep impression on both of us.

"Welcome, everyone," Jeff Fountain, the base leader and YWAM coordinator, began. "Tonight we have a special guest, all the way from Brazil."

Elated, I elbowed Johan, whose eyes were fixed on the young Brazilian who, with one leap, mounted the podium. The young man spoke English, which was translated into Dutch, and painted a vivid picture of his enormous country, the size of Europe. He described the 150 unreached Indian tribes in the jungles of the Amazon region, his country's gigantic economic problems, the slum areas in the big cities, and the six million abandoned, forgotten street children.

As my heart skipped a beat, I squeezed Johan's hand.

"With luck," the speaker continued, "these children each have their own torn, dirty blanket or perhaps a cardboard box to sleep in. The street has become their home. That is all they know."

I thought of the wicker bassinet with its soft, blue blanket in the corner of our room and gently patted my swollen belly.

The meeting lasted over two hours, but time flew by as we tried to digest everything we heard about those street children. When the speaker finally finished, I heaved a deep sigh and leaned over to Johan. "Could this be what God wants from us? To help those children in Brazil?"

Johan shrugged and whispered, "This is only our second month. I'm sure there's much more to come. Let's wait and see."

Jeff had taken over the meeting again and in his broken Dutch prayed, "Lord, we want to hold these children up to You and ask that You send people over who are willing to help them."

Johan squeezed my hand. We still didn't know exactly what the Lord had in store for us, but the conviction that He wanted to use us in missions was steadily growing.

After the lecture Johan had to pull me up from the easy chair I had been given. My abdomen had grown enormously, but I felt fine and participated in every activity. The foreign students looked surprised when Johan and I made little excursions on our tandem bike so late in my pregnancy, but I loved these outings. The reddish purple heather and the brilliant fall colors of the forest around Heidebeek were breathtaking. Besides, daily bike rides are routine for nearly everyone in Holland.

We had hoped our first baby would be born right in our little room at the base. On November 19 labor pains started at two in the morning. Soon the contractions became stronger, but the baby didn't budge. That morning the midwife came by several times while the students started a special prayer meeting for me. When she returned at four in the afternoon and the situation had not changed, she decided I had better go to the hospital.

I had been at peace the entire day and even now was very much aware of God's presence. Leisurely I got my things together, pausing now and then to "catch" a pain, just as I had told countless women to do during my nursing days in the hospital. Johan paced and took deep breaths with me during every contraction. Finally my bag was packed. We walked to the car, but before we got in, Johan put his arm around me and prayed for the safety of our baby. The way he peeled off out of the driveway and then careened onto the highway made we wonder whether his prayer had been for the baby's delivery or for his driving. We made it safely to the hospital, and that evening at ten, our son Pieter made his debut, weighing in at nine pounds. I was discharged the next day. At the base we were inundated with visits from family, friends, and students.

Secretly I had entertained some doubts about keeping a baby in a place that housed so many people and provided so little privacy. However, it didn't take me long to appreciate the blessing of living under one roof with so many experienced mothers and willing baby-sitters. Pieter was a great baby and attended classes with us. The louder we sang before each lecture, the quicker he fell asleep. Johan was a very proud daddy, who quickly mastered the art of changing diapers. Everywhere he went, he carried his son with him in a sling. I couldn't thank God enough for our little miracle with all those tiny toes and fingers.

ALTHOUGH we were learning a wealth of new things during the DTS training, we still weren't quite sure which direction God was leading us. Did He really want us to be missionaries? Five months into the course we began to get a little uneasy. There was only one month of theory left, then a three-month practical trip, which we were to take in Greece.

One of the teachers that month was a YWAM staff worker from Hong Kong. He related fascinating details about the work in Asia, and when he spoke about the children in India, we vividly recalled the man from Brazil. Shocked, we listened as he described the incredible poverty in that vast country and the unbelievable hardship children were exposed to if their parents happened to be poor.

"Often parents mutilate their children on purpose so that the children can beg and people will feel sorry for them," he said. "However, that's nothing compared to the tragedy of the thousands of young girls who are sold and transported to large cities where they are mistreated and forced into prostitution."

The entire class sat in shocked silence. I shuddered. Johan, a fixed stare on his face, didn't move. The speaker interrupted himself. "Let's pray right now. I believe God has people in this room He is calling to work with these children so that the light of the Lord Jesus can shine in their darkness."

Our heads jerked to attention. The speaker paused. We bowed our heads and closed our eyes. What happened next I can still hardly believe.

The children in Brazil! I heard an inner voice say. Was this God speaking to me?

"If there is someone here whom God is calling, would you please stand?" the speaker continued.

Stand up for the children in Brazil, came that clear voice again.

Lord, is that really You? I prayed softly. I felt Johan next to me rise to his feet.

Lord, do you see that? That's my husband. He's standing up for the children in India. What are You doing, Lord?"

God spoke again. *Go ahead and stand up for the children in Brazil.*

It was so clear, I automatically rose to my feet. Johan gave me a quick glance before he closed his eyes again. The speaker launched into a long prayer, but I couldn't focus on his words. Mixed emotions crowded my head. Was this what we had been waiting for—a clear sign from God of what He had in mind for us? Was He going to send us to two different continents? Does God break up families? I looked at our baby, peacefully asleep in his little basket at my feet. Confusion reigned. Even Johan uneasily shuffled his feet.

"Amen," the speaker finally finished.

Immediately Johan turned to me. "Why did you stand up?" he whispered, tension in his voice.

Surprised, I looked at him but didn't dare tell the truth yet.

"I stood up for a different country," he continued.

My heart skipped a beat. I held my breath and waited.

"I stood up for the children in Brazil," he said.

Relief flooded my soul. "So did I!"

God had spoken! And He had spoken to both of us! We were going together—to the children in Brazil! Johan hugged me tightly. We still had a lot of questions, but we knew we were headed in the right direction.

That afternoon Johan and some other students put up six large tents in our meeting hall to see if they were in good shape. To begin our three months of practical service, our class was going to Greece to attend a conference with four hundred other students from YWAM bases all over Europe. Once there, we would split up into teams to share the gospel with the citizens of Athens.

I had heard that Greece didn't have disposable diapers, so I bought eighteen large boxes. The leader in charge of the trip couldn't believe his eyes when he saw me arrive with all those armloads full. The next day he announced that everyone could take only *one* suitcase. Anything more than that wouldn't fit on the chartered bus that was to take us to Greece. I sighed and suspected that he had heard about our loaded-down car and trailer when we arrived.

While preparing for the next phase of our DTS, Johan and I talked about the children of Brazil with different leaders at the base and continued to pray. Even though we were both convinced that God had spoken to us, we weren't sure what to do next. Did YWAM already have a base in Brazil? If so, was it involved in children's ministry? If not, were we supposed to start one ourselves? We didn't feel prepared and asked the leaders if we could spend another year at the base in Heerde after our trip to Greece to get more experience and learn more about the Youth With A Mission programs.

"We have prayed about this matter in depth," the base director told us, "but we feel God wants to prepare you somewhere else for Brazil. We believe you are not to come back here to the base." He gave us an encouraging smile. "God will show you what to do next."

Feeling defeated, we looked at each other. Now what? Coming back to the base in Heerde had seemed such a sensible plan: we knew the leaders, could learn a lot from them, and felt very much at home here. Was God going to send us to another base in a different country?

"Just go on to Greece," the leaders advised. "God is faithful. He will prepare you in the right location for the work in Brazil. He will guide you."

"And what if He doesn't?" I asked Johan as soon as we were alone.

Johan frowned and didn't answer.

FIVE

In the Belly of a Fish

THE bus trip to Camp Lutza, a large campground just outside Athens, took four days. Traveling with a baby on this long ride was easier than we had anticipated. Pieter slept most of the time and, as long as he got his bottle on time, was a contented child. The tent assigned to us at Camp Lutza was barely large enough for our air mattress and travel bassinet.

"Do you realize this is now our only home?" Johan asked me. "I mean, we're not just camping out here. We don't have our apartment in Dordrecht anymore, and we gave up our room at the base in Heerde, so this is it."

He was right. We had stored a lot of our stuff in boxes in my parents' attic but had no place we could call home. Although we had been limited to one suitcase each on this trip to Greece, I had managed to fit in our blue crocheted curtains, which I suspended across the plastic tent window with a few safety pins. This made our new abode official.

Busloads of people arrived from many different countries, and within a few days the campground was busy with activity. Students from different nations freely mingled, and soon, in spite of the cultural differences, we all felt an overall unity among this large, diverse group of people. We had come to tell the citizens of Athens about God, and we couldn't wait to get going.

After two weeks of training we were ready. The plan was to spread out to street corners and city squares and get people's attention with our well-rehearsed mimes and then share the gospel. Our team leader in the meantime had located a rundown hotel in a dubious downtown district with room for fifty-six people, though ninety-six of us moved in. The hotel was a ramshackle, neglected building, with slanting floors and doors that wouldn't close. The owner had named the establishment the Dizzy Chicken and had placed a large sign above the entrance portraying a very sick and giddy chicken. Johan and I were allotted a small room on the first floor. The rest of the students were housed in various other buildings.

Accommodations notwithstanding, we had a great time! Every night at eight we assembled on the large balcony that ran across the entire front of the building. We had discovered that the evening hours were best for getting people's attention. Before leaving we prayed for the activities planned for that night. Usually we dispersed to city squares and street corners to sing or perform mimes, followed by a gospel message. However, some nights we took prayer walks or went out in pairs to personally explain the gospel to people. We often returned to our hotel in the wee hours of the morning, tired but with many exciting stories to tell.

After six weeks in Greece we were beginning to feel a little unsure whenever we thought about our future. We felt that if God had a place for us where He would prepare us for our work in Brazil, He had better show us soon, as we had only another six weeks left in Athens.

That week it would be our turn to visit the YWAM ship docked near Athens. The ship, the *Anastasis,* was anchored in the Bay of Elefsis and was undergoing a complete overhaul. The idea was to eventually use this vessel for evangelism and distribution of food and other supplies to needy nations around the world. The *Anastasis* had five huge holds for storage and even a small hospital. With its eight decks, it could easily accommodate 675 people. Our group of 450 students had been divided into groups of thirty, and every day one group was assigned to spend a day on board. When it was our turn, we were given a guided tour through the entire ship—and were sorely disappointed. Was this the great ship we had heard so much about during our Discipleship Training School? The *Anastasis* was old and rusty and in great need of a paint job. Inside it was dark and cold.

"Hi, Johan! Wouldn't you like to work here?" one of our fellow students laughed, slapping Johan on the shoulder.

"Me? No way!" was his immediate response. We had heard that the ship was nicknamed the Pressure Cooker because of the high levels of stress her crew had to work under. The crew lived on board and were pretty much isolated from civilization. The only contact with the shore was a small ferry that came by three times a day. The forty crew members were mostly in their early twenties and included some young families.

The whole gigantic project was obviously in its pioneer stages. It was poorly funded, there was little food available, and much work had yet to be done, not the least of which was scraping off tons and tons of rust. The *Anastasis* was not able to sail under her own steam, and it would be quite a while before she would be seaworthy. This was definitely not the kind of environment *we* had in mind to prepare us to serve the Lord.

Just as our group was having tea on one of the decks, the purser appeared with the warning that we had to get off the ship right away, as a big storm front was approaching. The storm wouldn't affect the large *Anastasis,* but the small vessels in the bay would not be able to navigate from ship to shore on choppy waves. As the purser spoke, strong gusts of wind were slapping my face and large swells were beginning to sway the ship.

With a worried look Johan peeked over the railing to the little ferry below dancing on the big swells. A muscular Greek sailor hung at the end of a rope that dangled from one of the decks. His job was to center the tiny ferry below a rusty ladder that swung from the side of the *Anastasis.* One after the other, students climbed gingerly down the ladder and waited at the lowest rung for a wave to lift the ferry high enough for them to jump. It was a precarious procedure. About twenty students had made it down safely and, hanging on for dear life, huddled together on the wildly bobbing vessel. We stood in line waiting our turn. I looked at five-month-old Pieter, peacefully asleep in Johan's arms. Johan, a deep frown on his face, looked up from the railing, shook his head, and said, "Jeannette, we can't do this. It's too dangerous. What if we drop Pieter?"

I shuddered. Just then someone tapped me on the shoulder. It was the purser.

"I don't think you guys should leave the ship right now. I'm sorry, but with a baby it's too risky." I was relieved he would come to the same conclusion. He cleared his throat. "I'll see if we can get a cabin ready for you. Wait here a minute."

We gratefully accepted his offer. The purser ducked into one of those long, dark hallways. Five minutes later a young woman led us through a maze of passages and stairwells to a small cabin for two.

"Welcome aboard," she smiled as she handed me a stack of disposable diapers. "God always has surprises for us, doesn't He?"

"Yes, He does," I answered, though somewhat dubiously, as I watched our baby glance around at his unfamiliar surroundings.

W I T H the gentle rise and fall of the *Anastasis,* we slept well and were up bright and early the next morning, ready to catch the first ferry to shore. However, when we arrived at the dining room, the captain in his neatly pressed uniform approached us.

"I'm sorry," he said firmly, "but you still can't leave the ship. The waves are worse than yesterday." He pointed to the small porthole, through which we saw an angry, dark gray sky, and continued. "The ferries don't even operate in a storm like this. You'll have to wait a little longer."

"But how long will this last?" Johan was getting impatient. "We have to leave this ship. We didn't plan on staying here at all."

With an understanding smile the captain shrugged and answered, "It usually lasts only a couple of hours. I'm sure the winds will have died down by this afternoon."

Afternoon came and went, but the winds didn't die down. They got worse. Even the huge *Anastasis* began to sway on the swells in the bay. We realized that even though we were annoyed and concerned, there wasn't a thing we could do, so in the early hours of the evening we retreated to our little cabin for yet another night.

"This storm lasted longer than usual. I'm sure it'll be over by tomorrow," Johan said, trying to encourage himself and me. But when we woke the next morning, we knew the waves were as fierce as the day before. In fact, the storm seemed worse.

"I've always enjoyed sailing," I commented, "but this is enough!"

We were pretty frustrated by now, but the storm forced us to wait yet another day. The crew were sympathetic, and several stopped by to chat. That night would be our third on the *Anastasis*.

"Do you think God has a purpose in this?" I asked Johan as we settled into our narrow cabin berths that night.

"I don't know what kind of purpose," Johan answered. "What can we do here? I am a teacher. We believe we are going to work with children, and this ship has a completely different purpose."

I agreed, and Johan fell silent, deep in thought.

With a sigh I turned over. "Dear Lord," I prayed softly, "will You please show us what we're supposed to do at the end of this month when our group returns to the Netherlands? We're running out of time here, and if You really want us in missions, You'll have to show us where."

Soon, I fell into a fitful sleep.

"HI, JOHAN and Jeannette! Have you thought about Jonah lately?" the ship's cook laughed the next morning as he served us steaming hot coffee. Surprised, we gave him a blank stare. "Well," he continued, "Jonah was imprisoned in the belly of a fish three days and three nights. God used a storm to point him in the right direction. We're also in a storm," he continued as he put some buns on our plates, "and this is the third day you're stuck. Are you sure God isn't trying to tell you something?"

There it was again—that same question. Surely this wasn't something the Lord wanted us to consider, was it? We laughed and assured the cook that this was purely coincidental, but in our heart of hearts we knew that with God nothing is coincidental. However, that day we could finally leave the ship. The winds had died down, and the waves gently rocked the ferry as we arrived safely on shore.

DURING the few weeks we had left in Greece, something strange began to happen. Every time we prayed and asked the Lord for wisdom and guidance, the word *Anastasis* came to mind. We tried not to think about the ship, but we couldn't get away from it. The thought came so frequently that we slowly became convinced that the Lord *was* speaking to us.

As the days went by, our attitude toward the ship changed until we couldn't wait to return and work on the *Anastasis*, though we had no idea why. Humanly speaking, it was not a very logical place for us to prepare for our missionary careers, yet daily we became more convinced that this was the exact place the Lord had in mind for us. God's guidance now seemed clear, and every day we became more excited. We realized that God, who usually speaks in a still, small voice, sometimes uses a storm to speak to His rather hard-of-hearing children.

Back at the Dizzy Chicken we prayed with other team members about this new direction.

"You know what?" one of the leaders said. "While we were praying, I saw a traffic light changing from red to green. I think you're going in the right direction."

His wife nodded. "Yes," she admitted. "I think that is right."

Excited, I squeezed Johan's hand.

The next day we mailed off our application forms requesting to work as staff on the *Anastasis*. After only a week we received a reply.

"Johan, here's a letter from the ship for you."

Quickly, Johan took the white envelope. Eagerly, I peeked over his shoulder as he tore it open.

Dear Johan and Jeannette,

We're sorry to inform you we are not taking on additional staff at this time.

Your brother in Christ,
Don Stephens, Director, Mercy Ships

Dumbfounded, we stared at each other. How could this be? We finally thought we had heard from God, and now the door was closed! Now what?

"Why don't we pray," Johan suggested lamely. But I didn't want to pray anymore. What's the use? Angry and confused, I stalked out of our room. Is this why we had quit our jobs, sold our car and motorbike, and burned all our bridges? Was it really possible to hear from God, or was it just our imagination? Was this whole group of over 450 people naive enough to believe in fairy tales?

God, where are You, anyway? my heart screamed.

I stomped over to the porch and stared angrily at the noisy street below. Endless lines of cars crept through the narrow street. Throngs of pedestrians scurried along the sidewalks. Suddenly I felt utterly lost and lonely in this big city of Athens.

I don't know how long I stood there, but the sun was setting when I felt Johan's arm gently around my shoulders.

"Jeannette, I prayed, and I believe God still wants us on that ship."

I stared at him defiantly.

"How can that be?" I challenged. "You read Don's letter. He said no, and he's the director."

"I don't understand it either," Johan admitted, "but I really feel God wants us to go to that ship. Maybe we should try to talk to this Don Stephens."

We gazed silently over the bustling city as it slowly faded into darkness.

DIRECTOR Don Stephens came ashore a few days later and met us in a small park near the beach. He was a tall, friendly man who, in spite of the heat, wore a suit. In his blue jacket with shiny copper buttons, he looked the part of a ship's captain. Smiling, he shook our hands with a firm grip.

"So you're the ones who want to join our crew?" he began.

"Yes." We told him our story, how we had tried to discern the will of God for our lives and why we felt we needed to join the ship's crew.

Don listened intently.

"We have a problem," he finally began. "To be honest, the ship's finances have all but dried up. We've been anchored here for a year.

Much work still needs to be done, but we're out of funds. Several crew members have already returned to their own countries. We're in a crisis and have decided not to accept additional crew members."

Don looked somber, then continued. "There's more. We're almost out of food and have just enough oil left to operate the generators a few hours a day for electricity." He sighed deeply and fell silent.

Breathless, we had listened. Was that it?

"It doesn't matter, Don," I finally explained. "We're not looking for an easy or comfortable place. We want to be obedient to God."

Slowly Don shook his head and continued. "You don't quite understand. Right now conditions on the ship are really tough. What if you can't keep up? What will your families say, and your church? It could do more harm than good. Perhaps you should wait a year. By then the ship will be able to set sail and it'll be easier to raise support. Who would want to support you while you're on a ship that's going nowhere? Besides," he confessed, "there are not too many people who believe in the future of this ship."

He pulled a white handkerchief from his pocket and wiped his forehead.

"Don," Johan said confidently, "we firmly believe God wants us on this ship as soon as possible and not after a year. It's not a problem if things get rough. We really want to follow God's will for our lives and believe we can tough it out."

Don gave us a long, pensive look.

"Okay," he finally agreed, "let's go ahead. Actually, it's rather encouraging that God is giving us additional crew members at a time like this. But remember," he stressed and raised his forefinger, "I've warned you!"

During the remaining weeks in Greece, we often thought about Don's words and wondered what our parents *would* think about our plans. We didn't have to wait long to find out.

SIX

God First

FOR many years, Johan's dad had been suffering from a spinal condition. Toward the end of our stay in Greece we received word that his condition had deteriorated. That came as a shock. His birthday was coming up. Would this be his last? Even if he made it, how often would we be able to see him now that we were going into missions? Jesus' words about leaving home, brothers, sisters, father, mother, children, and possessions for the love of the gospel burned deep in our hearts. Leaving members of your family when they are healthy is one thing, but when they are ill or, as in the case of my sister Carla and her husband, Sieb, they don't know the Lord, it's quite another. While agonizing over these questions during the coming months, we would be severely tested.

We decided to return to Holland before joining the ship, and instead of taking the long bus ride, we flew back. Johan's father, who had been a lively and fairly active man, now sat slumped in a wheelchair, his once expressive hands quietly folded in his lap. We were deeply grieved to see him this way. Only his blue eyes, greatly magnified behind thick glasses, hinted that he was still the same man—a father interested in everything we did and deeply concerned about our future.

"Dad, we believe God has called us to work on the *Anastasis* in preparation for the work with street children in Brazil." Johan's voice was tense, his face serious. He knew his father had great expectations for him, but not this kind.

Johan and his ten brothers and sisters had been taken to church from the age of two where their dad, the only elder in the small village church without a pastor, would read sermons every Sunday and then teach Sunday school to all the children. Johan's dad was a master storyteller and always held the children's attention. To this day, Johan vividly recalls the many Bible stories his dad so eloquently brought to life. When Johan was a small child, his dad even took him to church committee meetings. He had often expressed the hope that one day Johan would be a pastor.

A long discussion followed Johan's unexpected announcement. Because of his illness, his dad had difficulty expressing himself. He had a deep faith in God, and his only desire for his children was that they, too, would know God. He told us that on the one hand, he greatly doubted whether we had made the right choice, but on the other hand, he loved us very much, and because of this love, he was willing to believe in us and trust that we had made the right decision.

During our short visit we had many talks and discussions with Johan's mom and many of his brothers and sisters. None of them quite understood what had motivated our decision. It was so different from their own way of thinking. We cared deeply for our families and didn't want to hurt them, but we couldn't change our plans and start looking for jobs and a home again just to keep the peace. That would compromise our obedience to God and His call on our lives. All in all, it was a very difficult visit.

Had it also been difficult for the Lord Jesus when He had to leave the safety of His carpenter's shop at the age of thirty? What had He felt when He looked into the anxious eyes of His mother, who by that time may have been widowed? I found it very hard to explain to Johan's mother that even though we loved them dearly, our obedience to the Lord came first. It almost made me feel like a traitor. Finally, with heavy hearts, we said our farewells. Perhaps it was the last time we would see Johan's dad this side of heaven. Tears blurred my vision, and Johan, usually not the emotional one, wept as he gripped his dad's frail body in a long hug.

When we got into the car, I clutched baby Pieter close to me. His trust in me was encouraging. I realized I could rely on God with the same childlike faith as this little child in my arms was trusting me— faith that my heavenly Father knew best. I lowered the window and waved until the two lonely figures at the curb disappeared from view. For a long time neither of us spoke, both lost in thought. To say good-bye, I read somewhere, is to die a little. How true, I thought. Soon it would become even harder.

My own parents were also deeply concerned about our future, especially since we would receive no salary or compensation from YWAM. In fact, the opposite was true—we had to pay *them* a monthly compensation for room and board.

"You know," my dad reminded us, "you'll never find a church who's going to support you. Who will pay your living expenses? Besides, you can't just pack up and leave; you have a family now."

He was right, since we actually did not belong to any church. We had attended services, as much as my irregular nurse's schedule would allow, but since moving to Dordrecht we had never officially joined a church. Most of our friends were from our Bible study in Gouda. They *did* stand behind us, but most of them were young, even younger than we were. Many were still students; others had just started new jobs. It was not exactly a viable source for dependable support. We had a small bank account, but what would happen when that was gone? We had no answers. My parents kept hoping we would change our minds. We were sorry to disappoint them and see the hurt in their eyes, but I didn't seem to be able to find the right words to convince them that we did love them but had to obey God.

"HOW can you be so sure?" my sister Carla demanded one evening as she put two mugs of coffee in front of us. We sensed that she was really seeking God in her life. Her husband, Sieb, also questioned us. We were sitting in their spacious, nicely furnished living room.

During the first eight years of their marriage they hadn't given much thought to God. Everything had gone well for them—a successful business, three adorable daughters, and a nice home. Once in a while they would go to church, but their faith wasn't a living reality. Their lives were too busy. That is, until a few weeks before, when Sieb's dad had died suddenly. This had been not only a shock but also a wake-up call, after which many questions about life after death had begun to surface. Carla and Sieb just couldn't get away from it, and we talked for hours deep into the night.

I was glad my sister and brother-in-law were finally getting serious about their faith, for I had prayed for them many times. Every evening they came a little closer to a personal relationship with God, but had not made a final decision to trust Him with their entire life and future. In a few days we would be leaving for Greece to work on the ship and tell the Greek people about Jesus, and here we were, sitting with Sieb and Carla, who were seeking Him so earnestly.

Lord, is this the right time for us to leave? I prayed silently. *My sister and brother-in-law need me to help them find You.*

No, the Lord spoke to my heart, *Carla and Sieb don't need you; they need Me.*

God had made it clear that He would take care of them and that my responsibility was to obey Him. Suddenly I was absolutely sure that they would find Him. I didn't have to stay in Holland to "help." My prayers in Greece would be as effective as they had been in Holland. Greatly relieved, we said our final good-byes that night.

This time we took the train to Greece. It was faster than the bus, and we could take more luggage than on a plane. I had run out of disposable diapers and resigned myself to cotton ones. Once again we were traveling with too many crammed suitcases, bulging bags, and heavy boxes. Johan laboriously stuffed some of the baggage under the seats in our train compartment and filled the luggage racks above our heads. When every inch of space had been taken, several large sacks with bulky sleeping bags and blankets were still piled on our seats.

Pensively Johan assessed the situation. I giggled and playfully put Pieter on top of the heap.

"I have no idea how we accumulated all this stuff," I said sheepishly, "but I'm sure every item will come in handy someday. It's all very useful, you know, such as our crocheted blue curtains."

Johan grinned and tenderly put his arm around me.

"Most of this stuff we probably won't need at all," he said softly, "but we have each other, and God has us."

He swung Pieter from his lofty perch to his lap, and with a feeling of contentment I had not known these past two months, we began our journey.

A young, tall American met us in Athens. He casually informed us that during our absence the entire crew of the *Anastasis* had been evacuated from the ship to an old hotel. While in the Netherlands we had heard rumors about problems with the harbor authorities, but this came as a surprise. While handling our luggage, the American said he would take us to the hotel and would pick up Johan the following Monday to take him to the ship. Questions immediately popped up, but I decided to keep quiet and wait and see. From the backseat of the car I watched the busy Athens traffic whiz by. Soon we arrived at an old hotel in a small fishing village just outside Athens. The ship's captain, a rather serious older man we remembered from our first visit to the ship, welcomed us in person. He looked worried.

"This is a difficult time for you to join us," he sighed. "Everything is so uncertain. We can't even afford to stay in this hotel very long."

His wife came scurrying down the creaky stairs and greeted us with a motherly hug.

"Oh, my dears, welcome! Did you have a good trip? I hope you did. You came by train, right?" She didn't wait for an answer. "I bet you're tired. We've kept some dinner for you. And…oh dear, what a darling little fellow. I hope you will soon feel at home. Let me get someone to help you with your luggage. Oh dear, oh dear…," and off she went.

In a fog we carried our belongings to our room. Yes, we were tired and decided not to worry and to get some rest first. Tomorrow we would find out what kind of work we were assigned to do.

The next morning, the purser who had spoken to us the first time we were on board knocked on our door. He explained that on Monday Johan would move to the ship with nineteen other men. Johan would work and live there for six days and return to the hotel Saturday evening so he would be free all of Sunday. Alarmed, I asked the purser, "Can't I come along?" I knew the answer.

"I'm sorry, that's not possible. Actually, the harbor authorities don't want anyone to live on board, but we finally persuaded them to allow at least the men to return. Again, I'm sorry, but women and children have to stay here."

Only in the gospel of Luke in the verse about leaving parents, brothers, and sisters to follow Jesus is leaving a wife mentioned as well. To leave your husband or your wife to follow Jesus had always seemed an odd idea to me, one that I had never quite understood. Wasn't it God who had instituted marriage? I needed Johan, and he needed me. And what about the baby? Here we were, living in a strange country. We didn't even speak the language. How could we be separated as a family right now? I couldn't imagine Johan living on board for the entire week and me and the baby staying here at this old hotel.

As the purser continued to explain Johan's duties on the ship, I mentally listed an array of objections. Quietly Johan squeezed my hand, then stood up.

"Okay," he said to the purser. "I'll be ready Monday morning."

He opened the door and let the man out. Bewildered, I looked at my husband.

"Let's unpack everything," he suggested with a shrug, "so I can pack my bags for Monday."

I realized it was no use rehashing what we had expected or wanted. We were in this together and knew that we may as well try to make the best of it. On Monday morning, barely able to hold back my tears but pretending that everything was fine, I bravely kissed Johan good-bye.

LORD, I can't do this! I don't like this hotel. I hardly know anyone, and I miss Johan! My face was wet with tears. We had been in Greece for two weeks. Every afternoon I put Pieter in his stroller for a walk along the beach so that I could pray. Every afternoon for fourteen days

I had burst into tears during this stroll, and every afternoon God had whispered to my heart that I *was* able to go on because He would give me the strength.

How do you convince God that you cannot do something if He maintains that with His help you can? I felt like Moses, who had objected when God sent him to confront Pharaoh. All my dreams of seeing people come to the Lord had evaporated into thin air. I missed my family, I missed my friends, and above all, I missed my husband. The job I was assigned to at the hotel—mopping the floors and hallways—wasn't exactly what I had in mind either when I had signed up for missions. I had longed to tell people about the Lord, and every afternoon, hurt and frustrated, I poured out my heart to God.

How grateful I am that our God is such a patient heavenly Father. Every day He convinced me that we were in the right place doing the right thing, only to hear me repeat the same litany of complaints the next day and the next. Finally, after two weeks, I was beginning to get the message and eventually was able to actually thank God for the hotel and our circumstances. If this was what He had planned for us, I wanted to be grateful and do a good job.

Johan was content. He worked hard and spent long days on the ship, but he also made quite a few friends among the men while I was finally beginning to make friends with the women. The only person I felt intimidated by was Deyon, Don Stephens's wife. She led our prayer time every morning. This was done in English, and although I knew the language pretty well, I couldn't get myself to pray in English. It just didn't sound right. Every morning I worked myself into a frenzy and was scared to death that she would ask me to pray out loud for a specific request. Sometimes I even practiced imaginary prayers in English in my room but still felt it sounded weird. It took many months before I dared open my mouth and pray in English.

Slowly we began to adjust to our new life, and when Johan was home we deeply appreciated our times together. Even baby Pieter did well with this new routine, that is until a few months later when he got a bad case of diarrhea. He was a year old now and eating solid food, including bread. Some members of Johan's family had a gluten allergy, and the doctor was concerned that that could be Pieter's problem as well. To make a definite diagnosis, the doctor wanted to admit Pieter to a local hospital for some tests.

I didn't know a thing about hospitals in Greece but had heard that mothers could stay with their children around the clock. That was reassuring. The fact that Pieter was a cheerful and easy child who didn't appear to be very sick helped me not to get overly concerned. Johan was still on board but, via the ship's radio, knew about Pieter's admission.

I arrived at the hospital with a mental image of a well-organized, clean facility, but when I was ushered into Pieter's room my heart almost stopped, and I had to swallow hard several times. Crammed into the stuffy, tiny room were eight beds, four on either side. Two tiny cribs had been wedged into the little space between the two rows of beds. Every bed was occupied by dark-eyed Greek children ranging in age from about two to twelve. Loudly chattering mothers perched on stools next to each bed. Actually, the din sounded more like an all-out fight with tempers at the boiling point. I was given a choice between the two cribs in the center of the room and chose the last one. Carefully I laid Pieter down.

Three children and two mothers started to cry. Several nurses and doctors entered the room to make rounds, but the noise only increased.

"What about me?" I asked when they came to me. "Where am I going to sleep?"

The doctor didn't understand my question. After some help from an aide, his eyes lit up. Aha! I needed a place to sleep? No problem— he had his own room right here at the hospital, and I was welcome to join him. He gave me a knowing wink.

Stunned, I stepped back and grabbed the sides of Pieter's crib.

"No, no, thank you. I'll stay right here with my son," I stammered.

What kind of place had I come to? The nurses giggled as the doctor shrugged and disappeared.

"The mothers sleep right here in the same bed as the children," one nurse explained in broken English. I looked at Pieter's tiny crib.

"Well, with mothers of small children this is a problem," she admitted. "But if you like you can sleep on the floor under his crib." I thought she was joking, but she wasn't, and when every mother crawled into bed with her child that night, I had no choice but to stretch my weary body on the floor under Pieter's crib. I was glad I had brought a sleeping bag.

"Yuck!" I sat up so fast I hit my head. In the semidarkness I had made out the bottom of the crib. It was covered with brown and reddish gunk. I felt my stomach churning. Hygiene had never been my forte when I had worked as a nurse, but this beat everything! Weary and depressed I climbed back on my little perch next to Pieter's crib.

Lord, I need You! I prayed urgently. *Please help me!*

Immediately, I felt a peace only He can give in situations we have no control over. Exhausted but strengthened in the knowledge that God was with us, I leaned against Pieter's crib and fell into a short but fitful sleep.

The tests took several days. While waiting, I took Pieter for short walks to watch the babies through a window in the nursery. One baby drew my attention. He had clubfeet and must have been at least two months old, since he was larger than the other infants. He giggled and laughed when we made faces at him. When the doctor made his rounds I asked him, "Is that baby waiting for surgery?"

He gave me a somber look.

"No, he's still here because his mother abandoned him. She did not want a child with a defect. That would bring dishonor to the family."

I was aghast. My mouth fell open, but the doctor had already moved to the next crib.

Lord, my heart cried out, *do You see that? How is this possible?* I had never seen an abandoned child before and was deeply distressed. Blissfully ignorant, the baby stuck his thumb into his mouth and went to sleep.

Tests showed that Pieter did not have an allergy, and soon his diarrhea stopped. Johan was able to leave the ship a day early to pick us up. Even though I was ecstatic to leave the hospital, the sight of that smiling abandoned baby with the clubfeet still weighed heavy on my heart.

Back in our hotel room a letter was waiting for me from Sieb and Carla.

"Jeannette, you probably won't believe this, but we gave our lives to the Lord and have decided to follow Him."

Of course I believed it! Hadn't the Lord given me His promise?

"We found a great church and will soon be baptized."

Beaming, Johan and I looked at each other. God had kept His word! We only have to do what He asks of us, and He will take care of the rest! Step-by-step we were beginning to know God more intimately and understand that He could always be trusted.

SEVEN

All Our Money?

WE WERE going to move again. The purser had located
a beautiful resort hotel right on the Mediterranean shore called Kinetta
Beach. The hotel, on the outskirts of Athens, had enough space for the
entire crew and their families. The cost was unbelievable: one dollar a
day for the entire facility. Why would they rent it this cheap? The purser
winked and in his New Zealand twang casually mentioned that a massive earthquake had hit the hotel a year ago. From then until today regular aftershocks could still be felt. Several sections of the hotel had
completely collapsed, but there was ample room left intact for our use.

Our family moved into a spacious room on the second floor with
a large balcony. The fact that our ceiling lamp swung back and forth at
times scared me at first, but then I got used to it. We had a magnificent
view—a deep-blue sea in front and a majestic green mountain ridge in
the back. Soon the blue crocheted curtains decorated our windows,
and we felt quite at home, although we all waited for the day we could
move to the ship.

The men worked long days on the *Anastasis*. Much scraping and repair work had been done, but because of lack of funds we could not get the ship out of the bay, which the locals had nicknamed the Ships' Graveyard. Most of the ships anchored here were dilapidated buckets of rust waiting to be sold as scrap metal. We, the *Anastasis* crew, contributed not only toward our food but also toward the oil to keep the generators running. However, because of the high cost of maintaining the ship, our food supplies were dwindling fast. Earlier, we had received twenty or so large plastic containers from the Netherlands, filled with outdated peanut butter. It was so dry and lumpy, it had to be cut off in big chunks that were served with a little boiled rice. The best food was kept for the men, who did the hard labor on board, but even their rations were almost gone.

One night when the men were home, Don called the entire crew together. In a serious tone of voice he explained that the financial situation was getting worse. He asked us to pray about this and write our families, friends, and churches to see if they wanted to send a gift for the work on the ship.

"But," he explained, "before you can ask other people to stand behind our work, you had better ask God what you can give yourself. You can't ask others to give if you're not willing to give yourself."

He spoke only briefly, but what he said made a lot of sense.

"Let's pray," he said, "and hear what God is telling us."

We all bowed our heads, and it was quiet for a while.

Johan and I had saved about ten thousand dollars, but the Discipleship Training School and our time in Greece had shrunk that amount quite a bit. We had figured that if we lived frugally we would be able to stay on the ship for another year. What would happen then was anybody's guess. I had heard tales about God's provision, but they all sounded a little scary to me. I believed that God could provide for dedicated, faithful missionaries but doubted whether He would do that for us. I was glad we had some funds left.

Imagine my shock when during prayer I heard God tell me we had to give *all* our money plus an additional one thousand dollars. Thinking I must have misunderstood, I closed my eyes a little tighter. The palms of my hands got sweaty, but in my mind I saw that same amount written in large letters on a blackboard. The image just would not go away.

Lord, You must be kidding! Look at all those zeroes! I felt panic rise inside me.

The amount didn't change.

Lord, You know we are going to need this ourselves!

The figure remained the same.

Confusing thoughts darted through my mind. If this was really from the Lord, we could never tell our parents. They would be convinced we had gotten mixed up in some sort of cult. The news media had recently aired a story about a cult whose leaders had extracted large sums of money from their disciples only to live a life of luxury themselves. How could we explain that this was not Don who asked this of us but the Lord? It seemed as though hours had passed, but it was only a few minutes when Don closed the meeting. Johan sat next to me on an uncomfortable folding chair. He looked at me with raised eyebrows. I didn't know what to say. What would he think?

Johan cleared his throat and whispered, "I believe God gave us a large amount." He frowned and continued. "I'm not sure, but He showed me an amount in dollars."

I remembered that my amount had been in Dutch guilders, so I thought, *I must have been mistaken, and of course my amount is way too high.*

Johan pulled out a piece of paper and started to scribble, converting the sum into the latest dollar exchange rate. I held my breath. When he had finished, I gasped and stared unbelievingly at the amount he had come up with. It was exactly the same as God had shown me.

With a concerned look, Johan asked, "Shall we do it?"

I got goose bumps and swallowed. "Yes, it seems to be really from the Lord."

I was grateful that God had spoken to us—to me, that was always a miracle—but I also felt as though someone had thrown me into deep waters before I knew how to swim.

Lord, please help me or I'll drown!

The meeting was over, and everyone retired to his or her own room. Johan and I slowly walked upstairs.

"Shall we pray about this again so we'll be absolutely sure?" Johan whispered when he had closed the door behind him, careful not to wake Pieter, who had been asleep for hours.

We prayed again and asked God if this was really what He wanted us to do. The Lord gave us a deep peace, and we were convinced that we understood Him correctly. How we would manage financially in the future was now entirely up to Him.

The next day Johan withdrew all the funds from our bank account. It was October, and we told the purser we would give the remaining one thousand dollars by December 1, even though we had no idea where it would come from. We would not discuss or mention it in our letters to friends and family. No one would understand anyway. God had told us what to do, and we had done it. Now it was His problem. Actually, it was rather exciting to wait and see how He would pull this one off.

The crew initiated a forty-day fast. Jesus had fasted forty days before His public ministry began, and we believed we were on the threshold of a great global ministry for the *Anastasis*. Our fast would last until December 1, the day a large sum was due to the harbor authorities. That was also the day we had pledged that one thousand dollars we didn't have.

During the fast, one small group at a time wouldn't eat anything for one day and would pray for the ship and the people we wanted to reach in the future. It was an exciting time. The harbor authorities constantly threatened to deny the men access to the ship and to charge us penalties. They didn't believe we would ever get the ship out of the bay. In their eyes we were a bunch of weird foreigners. Who could blame them? Except for the captain and chief machinist, most of the crew were unfamiliar with any aspect of navigation.

Ordinarily, ships receive their fuel from large oil tankers that come alongside them to fill their tanks. Not so with us. We were so short of cash that the machinist, armed with large jerry cans, hiked every day to the nearest gas station to buy fuel. It was a strange sight, and we quickly became the laughingstock of the men on other ships. Besides, the ship had been anchored at the Graveyard for two years and was still unable to sail.

Nevertheless, God had said that He was going to use the ship. The YWAM leaders had learned some hard lessons two years earlier when God had led them to buy this ship. Now we, the crew, had much to learn. We knew it would have been easy for God to get the *Anastasis* seaworthy, but we sincerely believed that it took all this time because we had to learn essential lessons in faith and trust and live a holy life before Him.

The generators functioned only two hours a day; the rest of the time there was no light or running water. The men diligently continued their hard work, but with dwindling resources it was getting more and more difficult. The weather also deteriorated. Winter was coming and temperatures were dipping. The cold and dreary, dark ship was depressing, but the crew worked with daily renewed hope and great expectations of what God would do in the future.

During those forty days of fasting, God gave us many specific promises that He would provide for our needs. One of the most awesome provisions came at the end of this period. That day most of the men were working on the ship. All the women met, as usual, at eight in the morning in the large dining room of the hotel for our daily prayer time. One of the dining room's walls was made entirely of glass, providing an incredible view. The sea was quiet, and some small white clouds dotted the sky. It promised to be a nice day. The beach was deserted. Suddenly one of the girls who worked in the kitchen ran in.

"Come quickly," she yelled out of breath. "The fish are jumping onto the beach!"

We had no idea what she was talking about, but others were already up and running toward the beach. Curious, I followed. Those who had reached the water's edge were jumping up and down and screaming with excitement. The day-care staff, where Pieter was staying, also came dashing out, followed by squealing children. From the window of the nursery they had also seen the amazing thing that was happening. And now I saw it, too: hundreds of fish leaping elegantly from the clear, blue waters right onto the beach. We could actually see them swim toward us and then gracefully hop onto the white sand. While the mothers stood gasping in utter amazement, the kitchen staff quickly got pots and buckets, and soon all the women and children, giddy with delight, were gathering fish. Pieter held on to my hand. We stood in the midst of all those leaping fish, and he, too, tried to catch a few. Some of the fish that we felt were too small we threw back into the water, but it was no use; they hopped right back onto the beach. We gathered fish in buckets, aprons, and bags. Everything we could find we filled with fish. The leader of our evangelism team, Alan Williams, who with his wife and three teenage children were part of the crew, burst into a song about God who wants to make us fishers of men. Still baffled, we joined in.

In all, we gathered 8,301 fish. The fish had beached themselves only on the small stretch of sand in front of our hotel. The beaches of our neighbors, both on the right and on the left, were empty. Some Greek fishermen who saw our miracle catch later on said they had never heard of such a thing.

God had greatly encouraged us. He blessed us with fish, and that day we prayed for a much larger catch of people. We prayed for the people who didn't know the Lord yet but who would come to know Him through the ministry of the *Anastasis.* We visualized the scene: the ship moored in foreign harbors, dozens of crew members going out to evangelize while medical personnel performed surgeries and treated people at the small hospital on board. The entire day was festive. God had given us a sign. He was with us. He would surely come through with financial provisions as well.

We cleaned fish until three in the afternoon. Everyone pitched in. At first I thought it was a gross procedure, but soon I was singing along with the others while cutting into the bellies of fish and then, with a hooked forefinger, nimbly extracting their innards. For months after that we ate miracle fish, superbly prepared by our Norwegian cook, who was an expert in creating innovative fish dishes. What a welcome change from the old lumpy peanut butter.

It was almost December 1. Every day we heard exciting stories from various crew members who had received funds through the mail. Our faith was given a boost, even though we were now stone broke and couldn't even buy toothpaste. Someone told me that you could brush your teeth with a little baking soda or salt. I tried it, and it was awful. We waited expectantly to see what God would do. As agreed, we had not written anyone about our dire need for funds, but every day I went over to the mail table with high hopes. I had no idea whom God was going to use to give us this gift. At times my doubts began to surface, especially as the deadline came closer. Was God really going to come through?

I had no problem believing that God would provide for people like Don and Alan. In my eyes they were heroes of the faith, but *we* really didn't amount to much. Would God really bother to do a miracle for us? I knew that Johan entertained no doubts, and I always tried to push mine away. *It must be the devil who wants to rob me of my faith,* I thought angrily and tried to focus on God's promises instead. But I started to hate brushing my teeth.

Pieter was now a year old, and I wanted to get him a pair of sturdy shoes, as he was beginning to take his first steps. However, for the time being, the little blue-and-red leather booties I had eyed so longingly in the shop window of the shoe store across from our hotel stayed right where they were.

It had also been weeks since we had had any cookies or snacks. We didn't go hungry, but this was our first experience with being broke, and it wasn't easy. Johan remained steadfast in his faith, and I quietly prayed that if God wasn't impressed with *my* level of faith to perform miracles, He would zero in on Johan's instead.

November 29 and November 30 came and went. Nothing arrived. We had decided to write the check for one thousand dollars by faith but had not received word from the bank that any deposits had been made into our account. Without a deposit from somewhere, we would be overdrawn. I had heard stories in which God had come through at the very last moment, so I was still hopeful, even though I had my doubts.

Then December 1 dawned. Today was the big day! Would the bank notify us of a one-thousand-dollar deposit? Or perhaps someone would give that amount to us in cash. Actually, we had figured that God would give us many small gifts during the forty days of fasting, but nothing had come in. Now I needed even more faith for the whole amount to arrive in one day.

I wanted my trust in God to be like a rock but was not very successful. Impatiently I waited that entire afternoon for the mail to arrive.

When it did, I quickly sifted through the stack of letters but found nothing for us. My heart sank. Now what? Johan didn't know yet. He was working on the ship that week. I had to stretch my faith to the limit to suppress a raw feeling of defeat. Frantically I groped for straws. Perhaps tonight during our weekly meeting someone would place an envelope in my hand and say it had been inadvertently picked up from the mail table, or… I desperately tried to think of other ways that God could still come through but didn't come up with any ideas.

At seven that night I was seated in the large hall and carefully eyed everyone who entered. No one approached me with an envelope. After the opening prayer, someone started out singing about our trust in God. Suddenly I completely lost it and hastily fled to my room. The singing kept going, and no one followed me. Everybody probably thought I was checking on Pieter, who was sound asleep.

Sobbing, I threw myself onto the bed. Where was God? And where was the money we had fasted and trusted Him for? Was it all a lie? I didn't know how we could go on. Should we move back to the Netherlands?

How I missed Johan! He wouldn't be home for another two days. I told God how very disappointed I was, and after an extended cry, tired and sad, I fell asleep.

The next morning I got up and mechanically went through my assigned work duties. After our move to Kinetta Beach we received more visitors. They were mostly the families and friends of the crew members, but we had also recently been accepting new crew members. I was now part of the small hospitality team that prepared rooms for the guests and new crew members. It was better than mopping the hallway floors, but I didn't feel very creative that day and forced myself not to dwell on our financial circumstances. It hurt too much, and my tears still flowed too easily.

That afternoon I put Pieter down in his crib for a nap. That was my usual time to read the Bible and pray, but that December 2, I couldn't get into it. I impatiently paced the halls of the hotel, eventually arriving once again at the mail table. Detached, I gazed at the mail.

Suddenly I froze. Wait a minute! There was a letter from the bank for us! My heart beat faster, but I would not allow myself a shred of hope. With clammy hands I carefully tore open the envelope. I didn't dare look. Finally I peeked and saw that we were not overdrawn.

Then…wait! The bank had received a deposit. But that couldn't be! With shaking fingers I pulled the statement from the envelope. The bank received what? One thousand five hundred dollars! Yes, there it was, in black and white!

Time stood still.

This is what we had prayed and fasted for, and we had received it, plus an extra five hundred dollars! Although the bank statement arrived on December 2, the deposit had been made in November. God had not been late.

Ashamed, I made my way back to our room and fell onto my knees. *Lord, thank You! Please forgive my doubts!*

I was speechless and humbled. The Lord had tested me. I had the feeling I had made it with a C minus, but I *had* made it! What a relief!

It was true; the Lord *could* be trusted. He *does* provide for our needs. God had sent us the needed funds on exactly the day we had written a check here in Greece, and He had used someone who knew nothing about our financial need and commitment. He had done a miracle. This was the God we were serving!

With the tip of my tongue I gently touched the back of my teeth. I could buy toothpaste again!

EIGHT

More Than a Thousand Words

ALTHOUGH I enjoyed my housekeeping duties at the hotel's guest quarters, I really looked forward to our weekly evangelism outreaches. Every Thursday the women went together, and on weekends the men joined the women.

On Thursday the women visited the gypsies who lived in tents not too far from us. The gypsies didn't speak Greek but spoke a Roman language we didn't understand. We took a tape recorder with some songs, followed by a portion of the New Testament and a brief sermon in their language. We also took them clothing. We had learned the hard way not to carry these items by hand, as they would be snatched from us the moment we arrived, after which no one would show any interest in the message. The women on our team now wore four to five layers of clothing, which they would shed only after the tape had been played and we had prayed. The system worked well except that we got quite hot under all of those layers.

The gypsies always welcomed us warmly. The women wore colorful but flimsy dresses even in subzero temperatures, and most of the children had on only tattered T-shirts. The gypsies lit fires right inside their tents, and several of the women had nasty burns. After they had welcomed us, they escorted us to the largest tent, where it took a while before everyone was comfortably seated and ready to listen to the tape. Then the older women asked for silence, and rowdy children were slapped to settle down in a corner. The gypsies always listened attentively, and their expressive brown eyes lit up when they heard the gospel in their own language. Right after the message they all chattered loudly among themselves, but after five or ten minutes it became quiet again. The gypsies asked us if we wanted to pray for them. I didn't know their language, but we could still pray, since God understands every language.

I often brought Pieter along, and his clothing was always scrutinized. As part of the team, poor little Pieter was also dressed in several layers, and with four warm sweaters he resembled a stuffed teddy bear. I had finally been able to buy him those cute blue-and-red leather shoes. He wore them the first time I took him along to the gypsies, and he proudly pranced among the other children. All the women were watching him. Most of their own children were barefooted. I realized again that we lived in two different worlds. My little son had clothes, toys, his own bed, and always enough to eat. Their children were half-naked, even in freezing temperatures; they had no toys, and they slept on a rug on the floor.

Lord, I prayed, *I wish we could do more.*

Suddenly I saw a scrawny little boy about Pieter's age. The boy toddled right toward me, then raised both his little arms. Carefully I picked him up. He looked so fragile. His mother joined us. She raised one of the little guy's feet and showed me a deep cut. Then she pointed to the ground, which was littered with trash. She picked up a rusty can and showed me how he had cut himself. The little tyke, with his messy curls and dirty face, squirmed in my arms. Behind me, Pieter was pulling on my skirt. He seemed confused that I was giving all my attention to this stranger. Suddenly I had an idea. I squatted next to him.

"Pieter, shall we give your shoes to this little boy? Mommy will carry you home."

I wasn't sure whether he understood, but he let me take off his shoes. At first, the mother refused to accept our little gift, but after I had put the shoes on her son's feet and he proudly walked away in them, she smiled broadly and spontaneously kissed me. There was so little we could do. I thought of all the children in Brazil and other Third World countries who were also barefooted. Wasn't there anything we, as Christians, could do? I didn't have an answer, but at least this little guy had a pair of shoes for the winter.

On Saturday night we took a bus to one of the red-light districts in Athens to evangelize. Alan Williams, an athletically built man, had a great gift for street evangelism, using lots of gestures to make his point. He always held people's attention. I loved to watch folks stop in their tracks, perplexed and intrigued, then stay for over an hour to listen. Sometimes drunks tried to break up our street service, but Alan, who had been a heavy drinker himself and was now set free by the Lord, was never intimidated. On the contrary, he often addressed these men, many of whom would end up on their knees, crying out, asking God for forgiveness.

Every Saturday night more people came to the Lord Jesus. One of them was sixteen-year-old Kostas. After listening intently for quite a while late one night, he had asked if he could visit us on the ship. Since he was a serious young man who was earnestly seeking God, Alan quickly agreed. Alan had sons the same age, and perhaps they could befriend Kostas. One day Kostas's father had dropped him off at the ship, and it wasn't long before Kostas had decided to give his life to the Lord Jesus.

We didn't know that Greek law prohibits proselytizing children. It's assumed that all children have the same faith as their parents. This posed a problem, since Kostas's mother was an atheist. When she found out that Kostas had become a Christian, she was furious and immediately went to see a lawyer. Suddenly negative newspaper articles appeared about our ministry. Even TV stations sent camera crews asking us to admit that we were working for the CIA and wanting to know how many of us were on drugs. All of a sudden we were the center of a vicious slander campaign. However, Alan, who now faced an investigation, wasn't intimidated and continued his street ministry with even more zeal, helped by a Greek pastor, Macriz. Kostas, who lived with his divorced dad, continued to visit us at the hotel at Kinetta Beach.

Right in the middle of this upheaval and the continuing taunts that the *Anastasis* would never set sail, we received a letter from my parents. They wanted to come for a visit. Alarmed, I wondered about their timing. I did miss them and would have loved to see them again, but I was also concerned about what they would think about our work. Would they be able to see as we did, with eyes of faith, a beautiful white ship reaching the poor around the world with the gospel? Or would they, like the people around us, see only a giant floating piece of rust with a group of nice but, at best, very peculiar people? I had no idea, but I was afraid that when they saw this primitive, pioneer-stage ministry, they would be even more alarmed about our choices. With mixed feelings I got their room ready.

The weather was getting colder. My parents arrived at the hotel, warmly dressed in their heavy winter coats. It was wonderful to see them again, and it was party time for Pieter to have his grandparents around all day as his playmates. We had decided not to hide anything and to show them everything just as it was and trust that they would not become too concerned.

My parents seemed very interested in everything we did and even came on board the *Anastasis* for a visit. We showed them all eight decks, from the enormous engine room to the two cabins that one day would be ours. Everywhere we went there was semidarkness, but they trooped right along and even seemed upbeat.

That evening, back in the hotel, Don unexpectedly called the entire crew together. He announced that the ship was finally able to move from the Ships' Graveyard to another bay just a few miles along the coast. For some unexplained reason the port authorities had decided that the entire crew had to move back on board for a few days. Loud cheers erupted. Everyone wanted to move back to the ship, even for a few days. Don approached us.

"Jeannette, your parents are not on the crew list. Would you mind staying here with them?"

"Of course not," I nodded, not knowing what loomed ahead.

"Gea can't come either—it's too dangerous."

Gea, another Dutch staff member, was nine months pregnant. She and I had become good friends, and I thought it would be nice to have her company. Her husband, Menno, and Johan had to move on board but could possibly come back to us a little sooner than the others.

The next day I was handed a piece of paper detailing how to reach the ship's radio in case of problems. Then the entire excited crew left noisily for the ship.

We had planned a few quiet days in the hotel with lots of coffee and Dutch treats. Gea's two little sons were playing with Pieter. A sixteen-year-old girl from South Africa, who had just arrived and was too young to join the crew, was busy in the kitchen. My parents were chatting with Gea.

Suddenly the phone rang. It was the owner of the hotel. He sounded upset, and I had to ask him several times to speak a little slower.

"There's a bomb scare. You have to leave!"

"A what?"

"A bomb scare! People who hate you called to say they will blow up the hotel tonight. You have to leave!"

"Leave?" I was stunned. It sounded so unreal. But the owner was convinced it was a real threat and had even called the police. The police, however, had informed him that there was nothing they could do and that he should evacuate his hotel guests.

I promised to call him back as soon as possible. Quickly I looked for the little slip of paper with the ship's radio information. I tried several times but was unable to reach anyone. Had they given me the right number?

Then I took stock. Here we were—without communication with our leaders, no car, and too far from the city for public transportation. Find another hotel? Easily said, but where? Besides, I had promised to stay in the hotel and watch everyone's belongings. What if these bomb-threat people had called just to get us out of the hotel so that they could rob us? I didn't have a clue what to do.

Slowly I walked back to our room and explained the situation to my parents and Gea. I also mentioned that because of our evangelism, we had made some enemies. They stared at me in utter surprise. In the corner of the room the children were playing quietly with their toy cars.

Gea folded her hands around her bulging belly. "What shall we do?" she asked.

Hesitating, I shrugged my shoulders. I had no idea.

"I'll get the girl from the kitchen and we'll pray about it," I suggested.

Lord, this is getting out of control, I prayed silently as I walked toward the kitchen. *My parents are here, Gea is nine months pregnant, her baby can come any hour, and we have three little kids and this teenager from South Africa. What'll happen if there's really a bunch of hoodlums who want to hurt us tonight?*

I tried the ship's radio one more time but still didn't get through.

Seated in a tight circle, we brought all our concerns to the Lord. One by one we expressed our faith in Him.

"Lord, You are almighty and all knowing; please help us make the right decision," we prayed. We took our time to pour out everything that was on our hearts and then waited expectantly for God to give us an answer.

The young South African girl opened her Bible and read the first verse of Psalm Ninety-one: "He who dwells in the secret place of the Most High shall abide under the shadow of the Almighty."

"I believe that means God will take care of us and we don't need to worry," she said softly.

I, too, had sensed His deep peace. He had it all under control. My parents and Gea agreed. They also felt God's assurance.

We decided not to move but to take turns with two-hour watches during the night. At the slightest sound we would wake the others. My dad insisted on being part of the watch team, but I convinced my mother to sleep through the night.

Toward the end of the afternoon, the front door suddenly burst open and in breezed Johan and Menno. What a relief to see them! After we quickly explained the situation, the three men decided to take care of the watches. Just before going to sleep that night, I opened my Bible. I recalled the psalm we had read that afternoon. Indeed, with God we would be safe and could sleep undisturbed. My trust was in Him. I nestled under the blankets and switched off the light.

The next day I awoke rested. Nothing had happened, and the men had seen no one. Relieved and thankful, we praised God. After a few more quiet days the entire crew returned, and our normal routines resumed. My parents said good-bye and went back to Holland.

I wondered why God had allowed them to be here at this tumultuous time. Would they ever stop worrying about us?

They did. From that time on they accepted the fact that their daughter, son-in-law, and grandson were in missions, and they became very supportive. Much later they told me they were very impressed with the general atmosphere and the love and respect the crew had for each other. But what had touched them most was the prayer meeting we had held that afternoon. To hear God's voice through that young girl and the scripture she read did more than a thousand words from us could have done. God had reassured them in a most remarkable way.

The Oceans in the Palm of His Hand

W H E N Pieter was eighteen months old we began to long for a second child. Would this be a good time to get pregnant again? Repairs on the *Anastasis* were almost complete, all port duties were paid, and it appeared that we would be setting sail soon, but would this complicate a pregnancy? We couldn't see into the future and wanted to be led by God in everything, including having another baby. We prayed about it, and after a while we both felt it would be okay. Soon I became pregnant. The conviction that this was the right time for an addition to the family would be important in days to come.

A few weeks later Don announced the good news that the ship's documents were finally in order and we would be setting sail soon. The entire crew erupted into cheers and whistles. The long-awaited day had finally arrived: we could move back to the ship. The next day was hectic. Johan, Pieter, and I moved into two small cabins, and soon our blue crocheted curtains went up in front of the portholes. We felt quite at home.

Our maiden voyage would take us to Los Angeles. We wanted to promote the ship and its purpose and fill the four large holds with emergency supplies for needy Third World countries. The day the ship's anchors were finally raised, many of the crew wept openly.

The trip took a little over a month, and during that time I felt fine. Others got seasick, but I, who had all the reasons in the world to be sick, felt perfectly healthy. I experienced God's protective hand on me and on the little life growing inside me.

We thoroughly enjoyed the long journey. For weeks we saw nothing but water, an unending expanse of gentle, bluish green waves. The water spoke of God's majesty. Doesn't the Bible state that He holds the oceans in the palm of His hand? I felt safe with this God.

In the port of Los Angeles hundreds of people crowded the docks awaiting the ship's arrival. Happy sounds of lively worship songs welcomed us from afar. Most of the crew had gathered on deck for this momentous occasion and joined in. God was good! He alone had brought us this far. The air was filled with high expectations. God had given us many promises for this ship and how He would use it to bless other nations. We were privileged to be part of the crew and to see His promises come to pass.

We had a fabulous time in Los Angeles. Churches brought truckloads of supplies. The Central American country of Guatemala would be our first port to take the gospel to, along with tons of seed for their fields, prefab homes, and even a fire truck. Then the ship would set sail for New Zealand to pick up supplies for the next mission trip.

Our baby would be due right in the midst of the long trip to New Zealand, and it would have been too risky to have a delivery at sea. We had a choice: stay in California for the birth and then fly to New Zealand or return to Holland for the baby's arrival and fly from there to New Zealand. With the high medical cost in the United States, it would be a lot cheaper to travel back to Holland. Besides, I much preferred to be with friends and family for an important occasion like this.

I had to fly before the seventh month of my pregnancy. Johan was needed on board and would follow a month later. Because all these trips would require a lot of cash, we began to pray for the necessary funds. One night Johan was figuring out our finances.

"Okay, Jeannette," he finally said, "we have enough for a ticket for you and Pieter, with one dollar left."

I breathed a sigh of relief. God had taken care of us again, even though we still needed faith for Johan's ticket and my maternity expenses in Holland. A few days later, with a bulging belly, a heavy suitcase, and Pieter strapped in his portable stroller, I said good-bye to Johan at Los Angeles International Airport. I was slightly worried about a plane change in New York to catch my flight to Amsterdam. The tales I had heard about New York didn't help, stories about penniless girls stranded in New York who ended up in prostitution rings. What would happen if I missed my connecting flight? I had only an hour and wouldn't even have enough change to make a phone call. My heart began to pound when I heard that my plane from Los Angeles had been delayed. When we finally got off the ground I was so occupied with my what-if's that I had no time to remind myself that God was in control of my life and had always taken care of me.

Our plane finally arrived in New York ten minutes late. I hurriedly pushed Pieter through the endless airport terminals. I had exactly fifty minutes to get to the international terminal. The airport was crowded, and everyone hurried in the same direction. I followed the crowd. After what seemed an eternity, I spotted a large sign with arrows pointing to my departure terminal. The arrows led to a bus. Nervously I boarded the bus, sat down, and stared out the window. How long would this take? Slowly the bus got into motion. I checked my ticket again. Yes, this was the right bus, and we still had forty-five minutes before departure.

"Mommy, I'm thirsty," Pieter announced.

"Okay, as soon as we're near the plane, I'll get you a drink."

"But I'm thirsty *now!*"

Impatient, I explained we would be there shortly and then he would get a drink.

But we didn't get there "shortly." In fact, after ten minutes we hadn't arrived. I kept glancing at my watch while Pieter informed me he was now very, *very* thirsty.

The bus crawled along. After half an hour, almost hysterical now, I pushed through the crowd to ask the driver when we would get there.

"We'll be there in ten minutes, ma'am," he droned.

"What?! My plane leaves in fifteen minutes!" My legs felt like rubber.

Unimpressed, the driver shrugged. "Well, that'll give you five minutes to find your plane, ma'am."

Pieter was yanking my hand. "I'm thirsty, Mommy!"

"Pieter, we *have* to catch that plane. When the bus stops, we're going to run real fast. If that plane leaves without us…" I didn't dare think beyond that possibility.

The bus sluggishly rolled along. When it finally came to a halt I was the first one out. Panic-stricken, I fussed with the stroller that wouldn't unfold. Pieter chose this time to start screaming. As fast as my bulging belly would allow, I sprinted through the crowded terminal, pushing a now howling Pieter, watching signs with arrows and gate numbers while Pieter's wails steadily increased in pitch and volume.

We passed a soft-drink stand. I grabbed my very last dollar. "How much for a Coke?" I panted.

"One dollar, ma'am."

I threw my last dollar on the counter, grabbed the cup, pushed it into Pieter's hands, and kept running behind the stroller. Pieter tried to drink, but the liquid sloshed everywhere. Finally, I spotted my gate. With my last ounce of energy I dashed toward it with Pieter still spilling Coke all over himself. The attendant was about to close the gate when she saw me.

"Wow, you just made it," she said as she took my boarding pass. "Go right in."

Pieter finally quit screaming and quietly let me strap him into his seat. Still shaking, I had barely pulled the seat belt around my enlarged waistline when the plane pulled away from the gate. Exhausted, I leaned back in my seat. All my pent-up emotions suddenly exploded, and hot tears spilled over my face.

Jeannette, I am looking after you. It was the Lord speaking softly to my heart.

Oops! I had been so consumed with apprehension that I had forgotten the Lord's ever present care for me. Ashamed, I looked at Pieter, who was now happily content.

"Thank You, Lord," I whispered.

S T E P - B Y - S T E P we learned to trust the Lord as a Father who never leaves His children alone. Johan did get the needed funds in time for his flight. A month after his arrival in the Netherlands our daughter, Johanneke, a beautiful, feisty baby with a shock of black hair, was born. We were totally delighted with our little family.

Meanwhile, the *Anastasis* had arrived in New Zealand, and a flight back to the ship for our family would be very expensive. However, it seemed that God was teaching us to trust Him for larger amounts. Hadn't He provided for us over and over again? We knew that He would supply our tickets. It seemed to be getting easier: the more we needed, the more we dared to trust Him for. In the future He would lead us to trust Him for things we couldn't even dream of.

Two months after Johanneke's birth, our family waved us off from Schiphol, Amsterdam's international airport. Johan carried our baby daughter in a sling. She was so small she almost slipped out. After a twenty-four-hour flight we were back on the ship. It was great to be home again with our old friends. For the next six months, the *Anastasis* made stops at fifteen New Zealand ports. Finally all cargo holds were filled, and with over six hundred thousand dollars worth of supplies, including 150 sheep (a typical New Zealand gift) in our freezers, we set sail for several Pacific island groups—Tonga, Fiji, and Samoa—all hit hard by a hurricane eight months earlier.

After we left New Zealand, we encountered our first hurricane, and most of the crew were seasick. I was one of the few who weren't. Grabbing the handrails in the ship's narrow corridors for balance, I gingerly moved from cabin to cabin to take care of the sick and give them little pep talks, coaching them to go on deck for some fresh air. Some folks were in real bad shape, but the captain had stressed many times that being seasick was no reason to stay in bed. Even the cook bragged that he had fixed our pancakes that morning while clutching a bowl in the crook of his arm to get sick in. I made a mental note not to eat pancakes again during a storm. As best we could, we attempted to get through our daily chores. I mopped the corridors and bathrooms and got several rooms ready for the guests we expected to receive after we reached the islands. Johan worked as a regular sailor in the maintenance department of the ship.

When after three days the storm was still raging, even I began to feel queasy. What also worried me were the ominous creaking noises of the ship. It was an old vessel to begin with, and even though I was not an expert, it seemed this storm could send her to a watery grave. Several times I clambered to the bridge. Mountainous waves pounded the bow and the front deck. That morning, Johan and a few of the other crew members had descended into one of the holds. They had found a trapdoor that had not been fastened securely and was leaking water.

A thunderous, prolonged groan seemed to break the ship in half. *Lord, is this it? Is this ship going to sink? Are we all going to drown?*

We had made a lot of plans, but did God have different plans? Amazed, I realized I was calm, and even though I wanted to stay alive, I left it all up to Him. I quietly told the Lord I trusted Him, whatever happened.

No one slept much that night while we were being tossed around on our narrow berths. The ship's magnified croaks sounded like a death rattle. Only the children weren't affected. Although Pieter and Johanneke rolled from side to side in their cribs, they never woke up. During those tumultuous days everyone prayed a lot, and when on the fourth day the storm finally let up, there was great relief among the crew.

Soon we arrived at the tropical island of Tonga and stood on deck as the ship was slowly towed to the dock. The bright sunlight reflected on the transparent water. Schools of brilliantly colored fish scooted away from the hull. In the distance, palm trees on a green hillside gently swayed in a balmy breeze.

The large crowd that had gathered at the dock burst into singing— beautiful sounds, very melodious but different from what we were used to. We realized that this was our first visit to a non-Western country, and we didn't want to miss a thing. The rich harmony of the music was already touching our hearts.

The majority of the islanders were poor. Every day the crew divided into teams and, joined by local believers, went to the streets to witness. Johan and I took turns. The docks were bustling as building materials were unloaded and hundreds of people waited in line to tour the ship and hear a gospel message. On our free time we toured the island to meet the friendly inhabitants. Surprised, Pieter pointed to some men.

"Mommy, why do those men wear skirts?" he wanted to know.

He was right. Instead of trousers the men wore brightly colored, flowered skirts. What surprised us even more were the people's homes, which had no walls—just a few skinny tree trunks holding up a matted roof. Children, pigs, and chickens freely scurried in and out of those homes.

In Samoa, our next port, we were welcomed by a group of thirty or so young people. They were with Youth With A Mission and had flown in from a YWAM base in Hawaii. From far away, as the *Anastasis* glided through the crystal-clear waters to the dock, we could hear their upbeat worship songs. Later we were told they are called the King's Kids. At the time, the South Pacific Games, something like the Olympics but among the Pacific Islands, were going on. Thousands of tourists had traveled to Samoa for these events. The King's Kids, together with hundreds of other YWAMers, were at the Games to share the gospel.

It was exciting to see dozens of people give their hearts to the Lord. We led several people to the Lord ourselves. What made a deep impression on me was a visit with several other nurses from the ship to a leper colony, where we saw people with all kinds of terrible deformities. We were given a whole evening in a small open hall to tell these precious people about the love of God. I noticed a sad-faced boy with an empty look in his eyes. During the message something began to dawn on him, and his countenance changed.

Right after the meeting the boy came over. "Would you please pray for me? I want to be a Christian and believe like you do." His face had come alive.

After we prayed I talked to him some more and could only guess at the depth of loneliness and isolation he must have felt as a result of his illness. But now he was beaming and, with both hands, clutched the New Testament we had given him.

"Thank you for coming!" he said. "I had no hope left, but now I know I am not alone."

He shook my hand for a long time.

Thank You, Lord, for allowing us to shine Your light into this darkness, I prayed silently. Even though we were unable to do anything else for this young man, we had given him the best gift of all—to know the love of the Lord Jesus Christ. I prayed for him often.

We also enjoyed visiting the local Christians. It was an incredible experience to be with believers from different cultures and different parts of the world. They serve the same God as we do, and together we could sing praises and worship Him. One day we attended a small church on top of a hill.

"Pieter, be careful, buddy. Hold your candle up straight." Johan folded Pieter's chubby little fingers around a burning candle. The sun had set, and one by one the candles were lit. The small, dancing flames cast long, moving shadows. The ship's captain and the local pastor stood side by side to break bread and pour wine to celebrate communion. Johan squeezed my hand. It was an unforgettable moment, and we were deeply touched.

We appreciated living on the *Anastasis* and always received just enough gifts from family and friends to cover our monthly room and board. There was never much left to spend on ourselves, but we were content to be where God had planted us. It had been two years since the Lord had called us to the ship. During those years we had learned many valuable lessons from our leaders and had seen the Lord do great miracles. Now God was preparing us for another change.

A Brazilian family had joined our crew. They spent several evenings in our cabin describing the lives of street children in Brazil. A YWAM leader from Chile told us about the enormous need among children in South America. Our hearts began to beat faster, and we began to pray specifically: "Lord, is this the time for us to go to Brazil? Is this Your time?"

A YWAM leader from Hawaii, Dale Kaufman, came by for a visit. He was the director of the King's Kids we had met in Samoa and had spent years as a missionary in many countries. He mentioned a course he planned to teach at YWAM's University of the Nations in Hawaii specifically designed for staff who wanted to work with street children. It immediately appealed to us as we vividly recalled how the Lord had spoken to us about street children in Brazil during our DTS in Heerde.

For the past two years we had learned much from the rock-solid faith of our leaders who, in spite of all kinds of calamities and roadblocks, never doubted God's promises. We had made wonderful friends and loved every aspect of the work on the ship. But now God was confirming that our time on the *Anastasis* was coming to an end. We decided to take the course Dale had mentioned. Hawaii would be the ship's next stop, and during the brief journey to the islands, we got busy packing our belongings and prepared to say good-bye to all on board we had grown to love.

TEN

"You Need to Go and Help Them"

T H E two cabins that had been our home for the past two and a half years looked bare. Our possessions were packed in four suitcases. Whatever didn't fit in we gave away. With some pride I realized I was finally learning to travel lighter. Carrying the baby and holding Pieter's hand, I slowly walked down the gangway for the last time. It was a hot day, and I welcomed the cool breeze on my face. As Johan lugged the two heaviest suitcases from the ship, drops of perspiration glistened on his forehead.

Many of our friends had gathered on the ship to wave good-bye. I felt a lump in my throat.

Thank You, Lord. We've had a fabulous time, I prayed silently. *Please hold us tight as we face a new and unknown future.*

A friend stuffed the other two suitcases into the trunk of the car that would take us to our new destination. I gently closed the car door, and as we slowly departed, I realized we had begun a new chapter in our lives.

"Here's your home for the next three months!" the YWAM worker who drove the car announced as he pulled up in front of a condo. We looked at each other with surprise. So far we had been assigned only one or two rooms at YWAM bases. Now we had a whole home? There must have been a mistake. The address was rechecked, but it was correct. I timidly inspected our new quarters: a living room, a kitchen with a fridge, and two bedrooms upstairs. Johanneke, who had just begun to walk, followed me upstairs. Pieter tried the faucets in the bathrooms.

"Jeannette! Look! There's even a drier behind this door," Johan called from the kitchen. I was already busy unpacking my blue crocheted curtains and held them in front of the windows.

"Look, Johan! They fit perfectly!"

The base where the course would be given was built on a beautiful hillside overlooking the vast blue-green Pacific. In an old shed Johan found two bicycles we could borrow. Johanneke just fit in the little basket on the handlebars, and Pieter perched on the backseat. We were in seventh heaven. Many heads turned when we raced at breakneck speed down to our home at the foot of the hill.

We had a fabulous time. During the morning classes, Pieter was in preschool, and Johanneke slept in a portable crib in the shade of a large tree just outside the classroom window. Every week we had a different teacher with years of experience in children's ministries. The lectures were excellent and gave us much practical insight for our future work with street children in Brazil.

LORD, there are six million street kids in Brazil, and we haven't heard of one Christian organization that is doing anything about it. What if we are the only ones? Where do we start? How big is this work going to be? I prayed. To help six million kids you almost need six million workers. These kids are wounded and need lots of help. My faith right now is not even big enough to believe You for a few hundred workers.

I was sitting on the steps of our kitchen door facing the backyard. The sun was slowly setting, and the palm trees had become black shadows. The boats anchored for the night in the bay began to light up. The children were asleep, and inside Johan was bent over his Bible.

Jeannette, I already have millions of people in Brazil. Was this the Lord speaking?

Lord, who are they? This was news to me.

The Christians in Brazil. The Christian families are the solution to this problem. A revival has been going on for years in Brazil. Millions of people have come to believe in Me.

I didn't move.

Jeannette, you need to show those Christian families how they can help and what their responsibilities are. Many Christians in Brazil are first-generation Christians; they don't have Christian parents, and they have no Christian education or examples. You need to go and help them.

But how, Lord? I felt very inadequate for such a huge task and afraid I would have to disappoint God. Suddenly I remembered something I had heard people say many times on the *Anastasis:* Do what is possible, what lies within your limits; then God will do what's outside your limits—the impossible.

The sun had set completely, and the sky had turned pitch black, but it was as though God had lit a light in my heart. Even though I still had a lot of unanswered questions and uncertainties, I had a deep assurance of His guidance. Filled with renewed expectations and trust, I prayed: *Lord, I want to follow You and do whatever You have planned for us.*

T H E course we were taking was expensive, and our funds barely covered the tuition. There wasn't much left for family extras. We became creative, and by saving some food and desserts during the week, we could peddle to the beach on weekends for a great picnic. Another popular outing among the students was a tour through the local chocolate factory, where visitors could taste free samples. We borrowed snorkel gear and explored the crystal-clear waters and swam among such a multitude of brightly colored fish that we felt we were in a tropical aquarium. We thoroughly enjoyed our few months in Hawaii. That is, until Johanneke got sick.

Johan sat crossed-legged on our "couch." Our living room had no furniture, but an upside-down cardboard box covered with a tea towel served as a coffee table, and our pillows and rolled-up sleeping bags became the daytime couch. Johanneke, her little face flushed, lay listlessly in his lap. Johan touched her burning hot forehead with concern. In the morning she had woken up with diarrhea, and now she was throwing up as well. She couldn't keep anything down, including the baby aspirins we tried to give her. Johan quietly prayed for her. It hurt to see her this way. We had prayed for her all day, but now she seemed to be getting worse. At first I had assumed it was just the flu, but now we felt that Johan should bike up to the base as soon as possible the next morning to get the address of a doctor.

That night we put Johanneke's crib next to our bed, but neither of us slept. Her breathing became very labored, and she seemed too exhausted and weak to cry. Once in while she uttered a pitiful moan, but every time I tried to hold her, she threw up. It was one of the longest nights of our lives. We had just prayed for her again and were tossing restlessly in our sleeping bags. What if she didn't get better? What if she died here in Hawaii? Would that make me bitter toward God? Would we still go to Brazil?

I used to think, rather naively, that God gave missionaries automatic guarantees, including good health. After all, I reasoned, He needs so many people to witness for Him, He would take extra good care of those who do and never let them get sick or die. Over the years, however, I discovered that that theory doesn't fly. I knew of many missionaries called by God whose spouses or children had died on the mission field. They were not rebellious or deserving of God's punishment. No, these were people who spent their lives in the service of the Lord. So why would God spare Johanneke's life?

I vividly recalled how I had fallen apart when the twelve-year-old daughter of our hospital chaplain had died in the pediatric ward where I worked. We all loved this man, and I couldn't understand why God had allowed such a thing to happen. The girl's small, white casket was placed at the front of the church with a huge bouquet of flowers entwined around her flute, her favorite instrument. I sat at the back of the church and felt as though the rug had been pulled from under me. It broke my heart to see the girl's father in the front pew. Someone began to play a melody softly on a flute. I heard muffled sobs and thought about all the plans her parents must have had for her that would never come to pass. Then someone began to recite a poem. It was about a God of love who had watched over that young girl and decided it would be best to call her home at this time. It so eloquently spoke of God's trustworthiness, of Him who never makes mistakes, and it strangely comforted me.

In the weeks that followed, the girl's father, a respected pastor, became a living witness to God's incredible love, not so much by what he said but by his countenance of love and peace as he continued God's work—visiting patients. His words of comfort to the sick were not hollow but were based on rock-solid faith in a loving Father. A thousand words could not have brought this truth home for me as did his life. Would God desire the same from us? My heart ached. Johan was still tossing, and I knew he couldn't sleep either. Without realizing it, we were both struggling through the same battle.

Lord, I prayed silently, *please help us to always accept Your will and not get bitter.*

Finally, Johanneke fell into a restless slumber.

With dark circles under his eyes, Johan biked to the base the next morning to set up an appointment with a doctor. I didn't leave Johanneke's bedside. She was extremely weak, and my heart skipped every time I couldn't hear her breathe.

"Mommy!" Her big blue eyes looked at me in confusion. I felt so helpless.

Please, Lord, help us find a doctor, I prayed for about the hundredth time when I heard Johan come upstairs.

"Good news! We can see the doctor right away. Keep her well covered."

I breathed a sigh of relief. The doctor, a tall and friendly man, immediately prescribed some medicine and said he felt she had a severe strain of flu. That evening, when the prescription began to take effect, our daughter looked much better and had passed the crisis.

"Did you also think she wasn't going to make it?" Johan asked that night after we went to bed.

"Yes, I was thinking the worst," I admitted.

Johan hugged me and prayed, "Thank You, Lord, for giving us Johanneke, and thank You that she's still alive."

WE FINISHED the theoretical part of the course and both got good grades. Now the whole class was to go to Los Angeles for four months of practical training. The Summer Olympics were about to start, and we planned to witness to the thousands of visitors from all over the world. We had much on our plate, as we would be in charge of over a hundred children and teenagers. We divided the teens among three of the King's Kids teams—just as they had been in Samoa. Johan helped the director, Dale, with the logistics. Pieter and Johanneke were too small to join in, but they enjoyed sitting in on rehearsals. After two weeks of practice the children were ready. Three teams spread out all over the city and performed in schools, hospitals, and prisons and on city squares. Everywhere they went, they drew huge crowds, who were often moved to tears by the spontaneous testimonies the children gave during their program.

What deeply moved me were the times we spent in front of abortion clinics to witness to, pray for, and talk to the women entering the clinics.

"Ma'am, do you know the size of a three-month-old fetus?" I opened my hand to show a tiny plastic figure. I knew this could be a shock, but that was the whole idea. These young women had come to the clinic to abort their babies, and many had firmly made up their minds. Our goal was to get them to hesitate and then to tell them about the love of God both for their babies and for them. We networked with pro-life teams, who would counsel these mothers to continue their pregnancies and tell them about alternatives to abortion. They would even help arrange for adoptions if the mothers agreed to complete the pregnancies but were unable to keep their babies. As a result, dozens of little lives were saved.

The owner of the clinic, who wasn't too happy to see us steering clients away from his clinic, came outside to talk to us. I was speechless when I heard him state that he was doing humanity a favor by eliminating unwanted children. He even told us about his plans to travel to India and Brazil as a "missionary" to teach others how to eliminate excess population.

I was shocked. Didn't this man know that God had created each child that he was prematurely taking out of his or her mother's womb?

Didn't he know that he was not really helping the poor by just killing their offspring? What kind of help was that? God clearly tells us to love our neighbors as ourselves by giving our lives, our goods, and our prayers—yet this doctor believed he was helping by aborting babies!

As the clinic owner spoke, I became nauseated, and when he said good-bye and shook my hand, I felt a heavy, black darkness. Quickly I pulled my hand back and wondered whether I would be able to do anything about abortions in Brazil.

The Olympics attracted hundreds of YWAMers from many nations, not to watch the Games but to take advantage of this unique opportunity to witness to people from all over the world. The national YWAM leader in Brazil, Jim Stier, was in Los Angeles and had made an appointment to see us. We were looking forward to meeting him, as we didn't know much about YWAM's work in Brazil and were anxious to hear more. Earlier, we had written Jim and his wife, Pamela, about our plans, and they had immediately encouraged us to come.

"So, you are the guys who want to come to Brazil?" Jim, a jovial man, warmly shook our hands. "Tell me, what exactly do you want to do there?"

With great gusto Johan related everything God had told us about helping street children. Jim listened attentively.

"We would love for you to come and start a work among the street children. We've prayed for that for years. Before you make a final decision, however, I need to tell you about our base. We have a beautiful plot of land we're building on, but we have no housing for you as yet, and there are no funds either. Could you bring a tent?"

Undaunted, Johan nodded. "No problem. We love camping, and we even have a small A-frame tent all four of us can fit in."

For a moment my mouth fell open—then I laughed. Oh well, why not?

Jim remained serious. "The base is still very primitive," he cautioned. "It's just outside Belo Horizonte, a city of four million. We have electric power, but it quits during storms. We also have wells, but in dry periods there's not enough water."

"God told us to go to Brazil, so I don't think that matters," I heard myself say to Jim. "Besides, your wife and five children live there too, right?"

"Yes, but it isn't always easy. There are no luxuries or amenities. Food is also scarce, but it tastes good—rice and beans every day," he grinned. "I hope you like beans."

"Like them? We love 'em!" Johan smiled. We all laughed.

Jim told us about an orphanage on the base with over thirty children. In the beginning, that would be our first priority. We eagerly soaked up his words and tried to imagine what the base looked like.

Finally, with a firm handshake, Jim left. "Let me know when you'll arrive at the airport and we'll pick you up," he promised.

Time flew by. In just a week the practical part of our course would be over. One day, with a deep frown on his face, Johan was crunching numbers. He sighed and closed his notebook.

"We have enough for tickets from Miami to Brazil but not from Los Angeles to Miami." Now what? Los Angeles and Miami are thousands of miles apart. Then we recalled someone telling us about people who leave their car behind when they move to another state. Someone with a valid driver's license could then drive the car one-way to its new location. "Perhaps there are cars that need to be driven from Los Angeles to Miami," Johan wondered. "Let's find out tomorrow."

"I HAVE two cars, a small one that's very good on gas and, over there, a very large one not so good on gas." The man at the garage pointed to a light yellow monstrosity almost as big as a hearse.

"We'll have to think about that," Johan hesitated. He pulled his calculator from his pocket and began figuring the total gas mileage for each car for five days and thousands of miles.

"If we take the small car, we'll save at least eighty dollars," he explained to me. "But the trip takes five days, and we have four suitcases and four carry-ons, and the small car has no trunk. That means that you would have to hold Johanneke on your lap the whole trip and all the luggage and Pieter will have to go in the backseat. If we take the big one, we'll have just enough cash but much more room."

"Can we spend the nights in a campground or motel?" I asked, looking at his figures.

"No, we can't. We'll have to sleep in the car. Shall we take the big one?"

I still hesitated, glancing at the yellow station wagon. I had never driven a car that large. Wouldn't that be difficult?

"Piece of cake," Johan replied cheerfully. "Don't worry."

He was right. The car was easy to handle, and we were glad we had decided on the big one, especially when we pulled in to park for the night. When the backseat of the station wagon was flipped forward we could actually stretch out between our four suitcases, even though Johan's feet stuck out the back. Pieter slept in front, and little Johanneke just fit on the floor between the brake and gas pedal. In Los Angeles Dale had offered us a box of canned food left over from the Olympics. We had gratefully accepted and learned to eat frugally.

Five days later we delivered the car, with no dents or scratches, to its owners, who dropped us off at the airport. We had actually spent less than anticipated and even had some cash left over. Relieved, we celebrated with a round of ice cream. In a few hours we would touch ground in Brazil. We could hardly believe it.

ELEVEN

Brazil at Last!

WITH a jerk Johan pulled our last suitcase from the carousel and stacked all our luggage onto a cart. We had arrived in Brazil. When I spotted Jim waiting behind the glass doors of the airport, a heavy load fell from my shoulders. I suddenly realized how tense I had been the entire trip. Tears welled up in my eyes. I could still hardly believe we had finally arrived in the country we had prayed about for so many years.

"Welcome! You're right on time!" Jim greeted us. How good it was to see him again! He guided us through the parking area to his small, yellow sedan and balanced our four large suitcases precariously on the car's luggage rack.

"You had better look behind you once in a while to see if we've lost any," he grinned. I trusted he was joking. Travel-weary, I settled into the backseat. Pieter sat next to me, and in front Johan held a sleeping Johanneke on his lap.

"It's about an hour's drive to the base," Jim announced as he started the car.

For a moment, I forgot my weariness and curiously peeked through the window. Everything was so different. On the rough road we passed a kaleidoscope of sights: homes with crumbled walls, women doing laundry, children in rags playing too close to the road, and chickens foraging through the dry, red soil around the homes. Men in their rickety wooden carts led by skinny horses swerved away from us as we continued down the road.

As we neared the city of Belo Horizonte (Beautiful Horizon), traffic increased, but instead of slowing down, Jim put his foot firmly on the gas pedal and drove faster. He must have seen my face in the rearview mirror, because he hollered, "Don't worry. Everybody drives like this in Brazil!"

With increasing alarm I watched the chaotic traffic. People crossing the street had to run for their lives—nobody stopped or slowed down. In the space of two traffic lanes, cars zoomed along four abreast. Would I ever have the nerve to drive here?

With ease Jim zigzagged through the melee. Once in a while I glanced behind me for possible flying suitcases but saw none. Jim navigated a sharp turn onto a much quieter road, which eventually became a sandy trail.

"We're almost there," he announced. Suddenly several children in pajamas emerged from the roadside bushes and came running toward the car. Jim hit the brakes and, grinning, lowered the window. An avalanche of unintelligible sounds gushed forth, and a flurry of little hands tried to touch us. Smiling faces appeared to jump up and down outside our windows.

"Actually, the base is another mile," Jim explained, "but the children have been waiting for you the whole day. They thought we took too long, so after their showers they came out here to welcome you." He laughed and shouted something in Portuguese. Ecstatic, they chattered back. We just smiled and nodded.

Here were our Brazilian children. It was for such as these that we had left our families and friends back in the Netherlands. For such as these God had planted a desire in our hearts, a desire to help them and tell them about His love.

Slowly the car began to move again. Squealing, the children followed. Some of the older boys tried to keep up with the car but soon had to give up. Johanneke had climbed into the backseat with me and Pieter, and she and her brother stared in surprise at the scene behind them. I hugged them tightly.

"We're here," I whispered with my face in Johanneke's blonde curls. "We're in Brazil!" I couldn't hide my excitement. Johan turned around and gave me a big smile.

The base consisted of a long, rough building with iron stakes still sticking from the roof, and various tiny homes with as yet unplastered walls, built haphazardly on a hillside, at the foot of which was a small lake surrounded by bulrushes. We were welcomed with great hospitality.

"Tonight you can sleep in our children's bedroom," Pamela, Jim's wife, suggested. "Tomorrow we'll help you move to the orphanage. For the past three weeks some of the men have been busy adding a bedroom, a kitchen, and a small living room for you."

I felt a warm glow come over me when I realized we didn't have to live in a tent after all. We were going to live in a real home! I felt like a princess.

Early the next morning several children came to the door to show us the orphanage. At first, Pieter and Johanneke were a little intimidated by all these children, but soon their curiosity won over and they happily joined them.

The orphanage was built near the lake. Our addition was built on the front. There had been just enough funds for the building materials; nothing was left for furniture, but I felt that these three rooms were wonderful. With the little money we had left, we bought the children bunk beds, and for the first six months, Johan and I slept on a borrowed mattress on the floor. Thankfully, I was unaware at the time that snakes would occasionally slither under the door.

The next day we began language study. Grammatically, Portuguese slightly resembles French, one of our required subjects in high school. In Los Angeles a Dutch friend had given us a twenty-year-old book titled *How to Speak Portuguese*. At one time he had toyed with the idea of moving to Brazil but eventually had settled in the United States. We studied six hours a day from that book, and a Brazilian team member joined us for an hour to answer questions and help with pronunciation.

We learned by trial and error. Except for Jim and Pamela, we were the only non-Brazilians at the base. On one of our first days a woman came to tell us something. We didn't understand her. She repeated the word *comida*. In our best Portuguese we said yes and thank you but had no idea the woman had come to tell us dinner was ready. When we didn't show up, she thought we weren't hungry and divided our portion among the children. That afternoon our stomachs growled, but we had learned a new word.

Our own children adjusted quickly, especially when, a week after our arrival, Pamela gave them a puppy. They had never had a pet before. The poor little thing was dragged everywhere, dressed in doll clothes, and made to ride in a buggy. Luckily, it was a docile little creature.

Brazilian team members came by for visits, and even though we could not communicate very well, we got by with sign language and quickly made new friends. Brazilians are very friendly and hospitable, and often one of the Brazilian team members would bring a glass of lemonade or some cookies just to show us we were welcome. My blue crocheted curtains were up again, and after a week, much to my own surprise, I felt quite at home.

Every day teams from the base traveled to the city to evangelize. Sometimes they went to a downtown area, other times to one of the more than three hundred *favelas,* or slums, in Belo Horizonte. Robson, the leader of one of the teams, described something that had happened two months earlier. He and his team had gone to a fairly new *favela,* which meant that the roads were unpaved and the "homes" were mostly constructed from pieces of plywood and plastic. Since there was no water or sewer system, the roads were actually open cesspools, which, especially during heavy rains, caused all kinds of diseases.

The team had found a small, open area near a large cardboard box leaning against a hovel and unpacked their guitar. With much enthusiasm they began to sing. Between songs, they each shared what the Lord meant to them. They attracted a pretty large crowd, especially children, who pushed to the front so they wouldn't miss a thing. To make more room, the team moved back a few steps, and one of them touched the cardboard box. Casually she looked inside and saw a little puppy. How cute! But that wasn't all—there was also a kitty and…what was that? She froze! A little toddler! Slowly, she bent over and lifted the grimy child from the box. The child's little head, covered with crusts and matted dark hair, was limp. Her big brown eyes were vacant. She was barely breathing. Quickly, the team member alerted the others. The children near them suddenly moved back.

"That's Dilma," they yelled. "She has scabies! Watch out!"

"Quick, find the mother of this child," Robson said. "She needs to see a doctor right away." He looked around for anyone who might know the mother. No one spoke. After some searching they found the mother somewhere in the slum.

When they asked her if they could take the little girl to a doctor, the mother said curtly, "No way!"

"But, ma'am, she's sick. She'll die!" Robson pleaded.

"No, I don't want you to," she repeated. She turned and was just about to walk off when she changed her mind.

"You can take Dilma to the doctor, as long as you keep her and don't bring her back."

Bewildered, the team members looked at each other. Robson explained to the mother that they wanted to help the little girl, but the mother had to take care of her. The mother didn't buy it. Robson tried to reason with her, but he finally realized that she wasn't going to budge. The team eventually took the very ill little girl to a doctor and planned to bring her back to the base to temporarily keep her at the orphanage.

The doctor looked grim. "Without medication she has two days at the most," he announced. "She has a serious bowel infection, and even with medication there's no guarantee she'll make it. She also seems to be deaf, even though I can't say for sure right now."

The toddler lay limp and listless on the exam table.

"By the looks of her teeth, I would guess she's about three years old, but she's very malnourished," the doctor observed. He rummaged through some drawers. "Here, take these. They are samples. If she's still alive next week, I would like to see her again."

AT THE orphanage Dilma was cared for with love and compassion. The first few days she just stared into space. Everyone at the base was deeply concerned, and many came by just to touch her hot little face with a cool hand and to quietly pray for her. Slowly she began a remarkable recovery and gained energy. Everything was new to her: the shower, toys, stuffed animals—her reaction to everything was a raw cry that soon changed to a high-pitched scream.

It was obvious she had never seen a toilet before and found it a very strange contraption. With a long, piercing shriek she made it clear that she refused to sit on the thing. Since she was still unable to walk or crawl, she just rolled off her own little potty when she was finished and shoved and scooted herself across the room. She had diarrhea and had to be cleaned every hour. Her high-pitched voice could be heard throughout the orphanage. From the moment she woke up in the morning to the time she went to sleep at night, Dilma yelled and screeched unintelligible sounds. The poor orphanage staff had their work cut out for them.

Dilma had been on the base for six weeks when we arrived.

"Have you noticed how tired and pale the staff looks?" Johan asked me one evening. "I think they're dead tired."

"Yes, I have noticed. It's not surprising. Dilma doesn't give them any peace, and I hear that even during the night she wakes up."

We were relaxing on our porch on a homemade bench made from an old board and some bricks. It was getting dark. Fascinated, we watched the dancing fireflies skipping over the lake. Our two children had been asleep for hours, tired after playing all day, a rosy blush on their little faces. Johan had his arm lightly around my shoulders. We enjoyed the peaceful quietness and felt completely at home.

"Maybe we could help them," Johan began.

"They need help," I agreed, "but we don't speak the language yet."

We spent a minimum of six hours a day studying Portuguese, and the rest of the time we helped our own children adjust to their new environment. There wasn't much time left to help out at the orphanage. Besides, we didn't yet understand the rapid speech of the children. Suddenly, I had an idea.

"Instead of helping out at the orphanage, why don't we keep Dilma here?"

Johan frowned. "We have only one bedroom and the bunk beds," he reminded me.

"Pieter can sleep on a mattress on the floor, like we do." I was getting excited. "And Dilma and Johanneke can have the bunk beds. It would be a great help for those girls at the orphanage."

"Well," Johan slowly admitted, "maybe it's a good idea. But she won't be our child; she'll still belong to the orphanage. What if we get too attached to her?"

"Maybe we can adopt her."

Silently we looked at each other.

"I doubt it. After all, she has a mother who will eventually want her back."

"Let's ask Pamela tomorrow what she thinks."

"I THINK it's an excellent idea," Pamela nodded. With a smile she continued, "You can even speak Dutch to her, since she is deaf."

When we told Pieter and Johanneke about our plans, they immediately helped to get the bunk beds ready and share their favorite toys with this small guest.

TWELVE

Deaf

DILMA'S big brown eyes registered surprise. We had taken her to our living room and put her down on the carpet. When she spotted the brightly colored toy cars and animals, she shrieked with delight. Even though she was three and a half years old, she could barely keep herself in a sitting position, and she more or less pushed herself around the room. She looked so fragile with her scrawny arms and legs and huge, protruding belly. Her thin, short hair pointed in all directions. Pieter and Johanneke dragged their toys in and showed her how they worked. Dilma was ecstatic.

Dilma's noises accelerated. After a few days we couldn't help but notice that the volume of her voice was still increasing and she was getting into the habit of repeating a one-syllable sound for hours, not because she was frustrated but because she was content. One day a coworker came by who didn't know that Dilma was living with us. When he heard those sounds coming from our bedroom he seemed surprised and inquired whether we had a parrot. There definitely was a similarity.

At first Dilma didn't eat much, but soon her appetite improved, and before long she was eating like a horse and never seemed satisfied. We had to get used to the fact that she was deaf. Out of habit we would call her name when she touched something she wasn't supposed to or talk to her while we were eating or when tucking her into bed at night. We hugged her a lot to make up for the lack of verbal communication.

What a lonely and silent world she must live in. To think she had never heard the voice of her mother. I began noticing every sound in "our" world that we took for granted. Dilma didn't hear the birds sing outside, the bark of our puppy, or the music from our tape player. Every night when I tucked her in, I prayed for her hearing to be restored. I never doubted that God could heal her, as I had personally witnessed miraculous healings after prayer. But as the days became months, I began to wonder whether God was going to heal *her* hearing.

Dilma learned to crawl, and soon she was walking. It was difficult to explain to her what she could and couldn't do, and we often had to follow her as she began to explore, since she couldn't hear us calling her. We often read to our own children, and I felt my level of frustration rise when I noticed that Dilma liked looking at the pictures but couldn't understand a thing about the stories.

"WE COULD take more children from the orphanage." Johan and I sat close together on our porch looking across the darkened lake. Carefully I took a sip of very hot tea from the mug in my hand and listened to Johan.

"That little room they built across from our bedroom would make an excellent second bedroom." With enthusiasm he jumped up and pulled me inside the house.

"Look," he pointed. "I could make two triple bunk beds along this wall to sleep six children." Since Johan had come from a family with eleven children, he had always liked the idea of a large family, but I had to think about this one. There were over thirty children in the orphanage, and I agreed that the five youngest could do with some extra attention. We could provide some of that just as we had done with Dilma. For the past two months we had studied hard and had finished our Portuguese textbook. We weren't fluent yet but could make ourselves understood. Anyway, it was about time we got more involved in the care of the orphans. After all, we had come to Brazil to work with children.

I was still gazing at the bare walls of the little room when suddenly in my mind's eye I saw those five new children sleeping under brightly colored blankets I was going to sew. Pamela agreed that it was an excellent idea. The next morning we hauled an old wooden table and some rickety benches into our kitchen. There! An instant dining room for ten. Everyone adjusted quickly to the expanding family, and Pieter and Johanneke loved all those instant new friends. Five o'clock in the afternoon was bathing time. Winter was around the corner, and the days were chilly. One by one I soaped the children up, held them briefly under the cold-water-only shower, and hurriedly dried and dressed them. Then Johan took over and, since we had no heating, marched them around the porch until they were warm. It was a precious sight to see all eight of them in their pajamas on the couch while we read them a Bible story. I felt honored to care for these children who came from poor and broken homes and to tell them about the love of God. Only Dilma worried me.

Lord, how can we ever tell her about You? She needs ears that can hear, I often sighed. Many evenings Johan and I discussed this matter.

"Do you think God will heal her?" I wondered. "What if He has different plans and she stays deaf?"

"That's possible. Perhaps we should look into learning sign language. Why would God heal her? After all, there are millions of deaf people, and maybe He wants her to remain this way," Johan pondered.

"But if God heals her, He would get all the glory," I argued. "Just imagine. We would tell our friends and family in Holland, and perhaps through YWAM, news of her healing would spread around the world! Wouldn't that be incredible proof of what a mighty God we serve? Who knows, people may even get saved when they hear it…," I gushed, "It would be a great victory for God!" *…and for Dilma and us too,* I added silently.

"But how are you going to convince God that healing Dilma is going to be a great victory?" Johan asked softly.

Frustrated, but at a loss for words, I just stared at him.

Many months passed and I couldn't understand why Dilma wasn't healed. We prayed for her every day. Was *I* the problem? Didn't *I* have enough faith? Maybe I needed to read the Bible more or pray more, or perhaps I had too much pride and God would use someone else's prayers. After all, we had been sent to Brazil to help children. Surely God wanted this child, whom *He* had brought across our path, to be healed. At times I felt like screaming, *What are You waiting for, Lord!?*

One day I was browsing in a Christian bookstore in the city when a large, yellow poster caught my attention. "Healing Service," the headline read in bold letters. My heart leaped, and I quickly scanned the rest of the poster. It was an announcement for a large crusade led by an American couple who had often been used by the Lord in miraculous healings.

Would this be it? I wondered. *Is God going to heal Dilma through the prayers of others?* Quickly I jotted down the date and location. The crusade was going to be held in a few weeks at a large soccer stadium.

We decided to take the whole family, and Pieter and Johanneke began to look forward to the event as well.

"Just think about the first words you want to say to Dilma when she can hear," I encouraged them. With high hopes we went to the crusade.

Huge crowds were streaming toward the entrance. In the parking lot we saw many wheelchair-bound folks emerging from cars. An ambulance brought a patient on a stretcher, who was then carefully carried into the stadium. This was the first time we had ever attended a service like this.

The stadium was packed. Johan and I held Dilma's hands tightly. With surprise she surveyed the crowded scene. We had been unable to tell her why we were here, and I could hardly wait to talk to her and explain everything.

The service was lengthy. The American couple read various portions of Scripture in which Jesus healed the sick. The children became restless. Then everyone was asked to form small circles and pray for the sick. I looked at Johan with alarm. Did we have to pray ourselves? We had already done that many times. I tried to suppress a sense of disappointment rising inside me.

"It is not we who heal," the woman on the podium announced. "It is God who does the healing, and He can do that through your prayer of faith."

I know He can, I thought, confused now, *but so far He hasn't.*

"Do you think they'll pray for Dilma?" I whispered to Johan.

"Please, don't bring the sick to the podium," the woman continued, "but pray for them in small groups." We looked around. Small groups of four to five people began to form.

"Let's pray with the people behind us," Johan suggested, standing up. I didn't know what to think. The children crowded around me. I thought the young couple behind us winced when they heard our prayer request for Dilma's hearing. We put our hand on Dilma's head while we prayed, but she didn't like that and kept squirming away. Her dark, expressive eyes questioned me, and her tiny hand held tightly on to mine.

Several people began making their way to the podium to testify about their healing. Confused, I looked from them to Dilma. Nothing. Nothing at all had happened to her. With an aching heart I closed my eyes. God was able to heal. He was even healing people right here, but not Dilma.

Lord, what are You doing? I prayed under my breath.

The meeting continued in a blur.

Finally, Johan touched my arm. "Let's go home. It's over."

We made our way to the exit surrounded by throngs of excited people praising God for their healing. Confused, Pieter pulled my hand.

"When is she going to hear, Mommy?"

Suddenly I felt weary.

"I don't know, honey. Maybe God doesn't want her to hear," I sighed. We drove home in silence.

I knew there wasn't anything I could do but trust God. Up to that point I had known Him as a loving Father who always knows what is best, but this I didn't understand, and it hurt. Valiantly I tried to forget my disappointment, and valiantly I threw myself into caring for our large and active family.

The ministry with the new children went well. Each child found a special place in my heart, even though Dilma's place was extra special.

I began to attend a weekly sign-language class. It wasn't easy, as my Portuguese was still far from perfect, and at times I learned to sign words I didn't even know the meaning of. The lectures were given by a deaf young man, and my clumsy mistakes often caused much hilarity. The signs I did learn I taught the members of our family, and eventually, with the help of a detailed picture book, even Dilma learned how to sign.

We still talked about adopting Dilma but knew she didn't qualify. The orphanage had no papers or documents on her, and her mother could show up anytime and claim her. I prayed this wouldn't happen, for I now realized how much this little girl must have suffered. She had completely recovered from her bowel infection and developed a ferocious appetite. I had heard that children who had gone through lengthy starvation periods lost their sense of fullness. They could eat nonstop, afraid their next meal would never come. I sensed that this was the case with Dilma, and we worked on that. She began to attend a class for the deaf in the afternoon. She loved it, but I couldn't figure out why she was gaining so much weight. I thought we had solved her eating problem. What I didn't know until months later was that the school was giving her two complete meals plus a snack every day.

THIRTEEN

New Life

"JOHAN, the test is positive. I'm pregnant!"

Johan was outside with the children hanging laundry on the clotheslines. Impatiently I pulled him inside. I had just returned from the lab where I had picked up the results.

"We're going to have a baby!" I pulled the white slip of paper from my purse, carefully opened it, and spread it out on the bed.

"There it is!"

Johan bent over to read it, then hugged me. We had prayed a lot about a third child and were ecstatic about this pregnancy.

Everything went well, even though I tired more easily and got irritated more quickly with the care of eight children. But my happiness about this new life inside me won out, and I was delighted when I felt the first tiny movements.

As my pregnancy progressed I began to be concerned about the delivery. With the other two children I had all kinds of help, mostly nurse friends. But what about here in Brazil? The thought of spending the first few weeks with a newborn at the orphanage, getting used to a new schedule and all, scared me, but I had no idea what else could be arranged. So I prayed that the Lord would give us a solution.

Among our new friends were a young doctor, Paco, and his wife, Annamaria, a Christian couple. Paco often came to our orphanage to examine the children. We had visited them at their home, and one day we ran into them at the supermarket.

"Jeannette, would you and your family like to come and live with us after the baby is born?"

I was stunned. How did they know I wanted to be in a "normal" home the first weeks after the birth of our baby?

Johan gave me a smile. "I think the Lord just answered your prayer," he said, squeezing my hand.

"Let's sit down and have some coffee in the restaurant here," Johan suggested, "so we can discuss it."

"I'm a little bored at home," Annamaria confessed after we were seated at a small table. "I prayed for something to do to help others, and you came to mind. I tried to imagine how difficult it would be for you to live at the orphanage with all those children after the new baby comes. We would love for you and your family to come and stay with us for a while."

I gladly accepted her invitation and while slowly sipping my coffee realized once more what a wonderful and compassionate God we serve.

On December 30, our little daughter was born. Delighted, I held her in my arms.

"New life," I whispered. "Let's always remember God's faithfulness."

We called her Michele. I was thrilled when Pieter and Johanneke carefully held her that afternoon in the hospital. The next day I was allowed to leave, and we moved in with Paco and Annamaria. It was a good thing we lived with them those first few weeks, for we soon discovered that Michele had a stomach problem and threw up a lot. It took me about eight hours a day just to feed her.

When after two weeks we returned home to the orphanage, all the children were waiting impatiently for us. A young couple from the base had been caring for the children while we had been living with Paco and Annamaria. Everyone wanted to hold the baby. The children loved

Michele, and at the slightest sound she made they ran to her bassinet, which, because of lack of space, we had suspended from the ceiling in our bedroom above our double bed.

Slowly Michele's stomach condition improved, but that first year I was often driven to near desperation when after an hour of careful feeding she would throw everything up again.

WE LOVED the work with the children and had begun to organize children's clubs for both the orphans and local children. We told the children stories, which we later typed out. Soon we had several small booklets in Portuguese that could also be used by other groups. We also developed some close friendships with Brazilians at the base and helped them organize a camp for teenagers.

These were all new challenges for us, and we were thrilled to see the children, step-by-step, beginning to know God. However, we still did not have any contacts with those homeless street children we felt such a burden for. That was a totally different ministry, and YWAM didn't yet have any outreaches to them. We often prayed for this situation, as did Jim and Pamela.

"I'm going to organize a three-month leadership course," Jim announced one day. "Maybe it would be a good idea for you to do the course. Afterward you could move with a team to the inner city and begin a ministry with the street children."

Our hearts beat faster. That's exactly what we wanted, although we had no idea how to start. Then one day Johan had an idea.

"Why don't you make some puppets," he suggested. "We can try them out on the streets. I'm sure it'll attract a lot of attention."

For a couple of weeks our little home looked like a sewing workshop, with scattered pieces of fabric, pins, wool for hair, and doll clothes everywhere. Actually, the puppets turned out to be big enough to be outfitted in baby clothes. When we finished we had produced six large puppets ready for action. The orphanage children followed our efforts with great curiosity and squealed with delight whenever another model came off the line. They were a great audience to practice on.

FOURTEEN

The First Street Kids

A FEW months before Jim's leadership course started, Johan began to take the red city bus to town every day to spend time with the children on the streets. He soon got to know many of them and listened to their problems, their fears, and their dreams. The children showed Johan where they spent the night and walked him to the fountains in the city parks where, if no police officers were around, they would jump in to cool off and bathe.

The children told Johan about their parents. Most of them came from one of the three hundred or so *favelas* of Belo Horizonte, slums where "home" was often nothing more than odd-shaped pieces of plastic held up by sticks. Most families had moved from the country to the city to hunt for jobs. They would often just claim a little piece of land in a *favela*, buy a few bricks here and there, and eventually build their own little home, one wall at a time.

When Johan went to the streets, he found the children always hungry and eager to accept the sandwiches he took along.

Almost all the children between six and eighteen years old carried small bags with glue. When they sniffed the glue, their eyes would glaze over and their reactions would slow down.

"Why do you sniff that stuff?" Johan asked. He got several answers.

"Everybody does it."

"I like it."

"It helps me forget everything."

The main reason was that it gave them more courage and made them less fearful.

"It's scary, you know, breaking in somewhere at night or stealing a watch from someone. But if I first take a good sniff, I feel better and I'm not afraid anymore." Or, "If I don't sniff, I'm too chicken to hang on to the bumper of a moving bus. I would be afraid I would fall off. But after sniffing, I'm not afraid of anything!"

A small boy who had just inhaled some deep sniffs looked at Johan and, dead serious, asked, "*Tio* (uncle), don't you agree I am the strongest kid on the block?" He jumped up. "Look, I'll show you...."

"No, no, that's not necessary." Johan gently pulled him down next to him on the curb.

"Tio Johan, couldn't we come and live with you?" Over and over they asked him the same question. "It's dangerous on the streets. We would love to sleep in a real home."

"Why don't you go to your own home?"

"Oh, Tio, my dad always beats me up when he comes home drunk."

"I have eight brothers and sisters and we have only one bed at home, and I'm always hungry. I have a better life here on the streets."

"If I don't come home with enough money I'm supposed to make by watching parked cars, my parents beat me up and send me back out on the street."

Johan went to the homes of several of the children to see their parents and assess the situation.

The children took Johan to the Rua Bonfim, a notorious street in one of the worst parts of the city, filled with brothels and bars where several gangs of street children had their regular hangouts. Rua Bonfim was a long, winding downtown street close to the large bus station. The homes were old and dilapidated. On the corner stood a large building with broken windows and crumbling stucco. Above the entrance, a large rectangular sign with heavy black letters proudly proclaimed this to be a seven-star hotel, even providing hot water.

A little farther down the road was a large fish factory. The putrid smell of fish scraps permeated the entire neighborhood. Between the old, paintless buildings were several vacant lots filled with piles of scrap iron, while heaps of garbage littered the steps to the front doors of the buildings.

One of the small bars along this street was a favorite hangout of the children where even the youngest ones could get alcoholic beverages. Stolen items were bartered for money, drugs, or glue. The bar was a small, smelly, windowless place about twenty feet by twelve feet. The front of the bar consisted of an old roll-up garage door that was pulled down at closing time. Inside the building was a tiny wooden counter, behind which rows of shelves displayed bottles up to the ceiling. An old, rusty fridge in the corner contained soft drinks. Completing the establishment were two small tables, each with four metal folding chairs. In back was a door, once painted blue. Although the door didn't have a sign, the odor made it obvious what was behind it.

Johan ordered a round of Cokes for the children who had joined him.

"We hang out here every day," boasted a ten-year-old. "But it's dangerous, you know. Yesterday someone was killed, and the day before two people died."

"You're kidding!"

"Really! It's true!" Even the older children nodded their agreement.

"About three children get killed here every week," one of the boys said softly. The man behind the counter looked the other way. Surprised, Johan scanned the place. He wasn't sure whether it would be safe to ask what was on the tip of his tongue, but his curiosity won over.

"Who were they killed by?"

The boys shrugged.

"There are gang fights. Sometimes the police get involved and take them away. That's the last we ever see of them."

Johan wasn't sure what to think, but it was obvious he had a lot to learn about these children. He decided to stop by this little bar every day and get Cokes for the children hanging out there.

Meanwhile at the base, four other people had become interested in working with homeless street children. They joined Johan on his daily discovery ventures, got to know many of the children by name, and visited a number of their parents in the *favelas*.

We decided to try out our six new puppets on the street children. In the evenings, Johan put together a rough bamboo frame tied together with old bicycle inner tubes. The frame was then covered with a king-size blue bedsheet. The puppet stage was super practical, light-weight, and easy to set up.

We taped various stories suitable for a puppet show and took them along with a cassette player. That way the puppeteers didn't have to memorize any lines. This was also helpful so that two of our helpers who were not Brazilians and as yet spoke very little Portuguese could partic-ipate. After the puppet show the team performed mimes in clown cos-tumes. Throughout the performance, the children remained spellbound. Sometimes we set up our puppet theater in the middle of the street, sometimes in parks or in one of the slum areas. On the whole, the pup-pet show became a great success and attracted dozens of children.

Johan told the team members about the little run-down bar on the Rua Bonfim and, after prayer, decided to make it a regular puppet show site. The bartender, who had come to know Johan, had no objec-tions. Still a little apprehensive, the team erected the puppet theater at the back of the bar close to the wall. Many children were present that first afternoon, and Johan greeted them all by name. He had arranged with the team that if the mood in the bar became too dangerous—for example, if a fight was about to break out or the police were on their way—he would ask the two non-Brazilian puppeteers to sing a song in English. That would be the sign to pack up and start praying.

A group of noisy children watched the preparations for the pup-pet performance. Some of them were drunk, others under the influ-ence of drugs or glue. It was stuffy, and the one bare lightbulb that dangled from the ceiling didn't shed much light. The two puppeteers, on their knees inside the puppet stage, were perspiring from the heat and their tense nerves. Full of confidence, Johan, after a quick prayer, started the music. The program had begun.

Right from the start the children were spellbound. They paid close attention to the story, which was about a thief who wants to steal people's joy and about the Lord Jesus, who wants to get rid of the thief. The children reacted every time the thief appeared. The kneeling puppeteers realized all was going well and were just about to forget their nerves and the heat when they noticed that their knees were getting wet. They were right in the middle of the performance and couldn't stand up. In the semidarkness they glanced behind them and discovered the source: from beneath the bathroom door came a stream of frothy, yellow "water." Gritting their teeth they tried not to get sick and managed to get through the entire program.

Johan didn't have a clue what was going on and cheerfully completed the program. With many gestures he told a story about the Lord Jesus and kept his audience's attention for another fifteen minutes. The shaken puppeteers hovered at the back of the bar with dripping jeans clinging to their legs. Then Johan launched into teaching the children some new songs. The children caught on quickly and were soon singing along loudly.

Everything was going so well that Johan completely forgot the arrangements he had made before the show. He enthusiastically invited the two puppeteers to sing some songs in English. Alarmed, the poor puppeteers became frightened. With knees buckling they stepped forward, not knowing what kind of dire calamity was about to occur. Their voices croaking, they managed to sing one short verse while waiting for the danger to explode. Nothing happened. Amazed, they watched Johan as he calmly closed the meeting and then unhurriedly mingled with the children.

Only then did the girls realize there was no danger at all—Johan had simply forgotten their code. Full of tears of anger and frustration, they would have gladly strangled him that instant. Instead, they packed up their things and then realized that they would have to keep those wet, smelly jeans on for another hour during the bus ride home. Poor Johan was still completely in the dark. He sat at the bar, praying with a boy, his hand lightly on the lad's shoulder.

Suddenly, both girls began to giggle. Here they were, thousands of miles from their comfortable homes, where they had left good jobs and had said good-bye to family and friends—only to find themselves kneeling in a filthy bar in a dangerous area in one of the worst streets in Belo Horizonte and drenched with stinking urine—all because they knew that the Lord loves street kids.

It was a good thing their mood had changed. When Johan finally finished praying with several other children, he noticed the bedraggled puppeteers, who told him about their predicament and how he had scared them out of their wits. But the girls graciously smiled at Johan when he asked for their forgiveness, and they cheerfully told him that when they saw the faces of those children he prayed with, it had made it all worthwhile.

Excited, we sent off newsletters to our friends and families back home. A Dutch Christian television network heard about us and asked if they could send a team down to do a documentary about our work with street children. The documentary would be shown on a children's program called *Hello Nederland*. Of course we agreed, and for two weeks a camera crew followed us on the streets and in the *favelas*. We enjoyed working with the television crew but had no idea at the time that the Lord would use this program on a far larger scale.

N E W help arrived at the orphanage when we began to realize that we would not be able to continue with our leadership classes and our street work *and* care for all the children in our home. We were entering a new phase and found one of the new couples willing to assume the care of our orphanage children. All, that is, except Dilma. After months of praying and seeking, we had become convinced it was not by accident that she had become part of our family. We didn't know exactly what it was, but we believed that God had a purpose for bringing us together. I still had many unanswered questions about the fact that Dilma wasn't healed but tried not to think about that too much. Perhaps her healing was still to come. I pushed back thoughts about her future care and the kind of life she would face with such a serious disability. Instead, I decided that if God had selected her for our family, wouldn't He also help us with all those details?

Dilma's mother had visited the orphanage several times and left two older siblings and a younger boy as well. She didn't want to look after them either. Even though legally we could now adopt Dilma, it would still take a lot of time and paperwork. After much prayer, including prayer with Pieter and Johanneke, we decided to make Dilma a member of our family. Meanwhile, for the three-month leadership course, we moved to another home on the base. Dilma, of course, moved with us.

More and more often the children on the street wanted to know why we didn't have a home in the city for them. We still lived on the base, an hour's drive by bus from the city. By now, we had been in Brazil for a year and a half. Would this be the right time to move? We often prayed about it. How wonderful it would be if we had a home right in the middle of the city where the children could come to shower, eat, and play, a home where they would hear about the Lord Jesus and perhaps would get off the streets permanently. Some faithful friends back home supported us financially, but that support didn't amount to more than a hundred dollars or so a month. It was not nearly enough to rent a home in the city and cover the cost for utilities.

Around this time a man in Australia, Jonathan, had a dream in which he sold his house and used part of the sale for the rent of a home for street children in Brazil. His dream recurred, and Jonathan realized that this was the Lord talking to him. Without hesitating, he sold his house and bought a ticket to Brazil to find out who was to get these funds.

We didn't know the man. We didn't know anyone in Australia. Jonathan had never heard of us either. When he arrived in São Paulo, the largest city in Brazil with seventeen million people, he asked some folks at the airport if they knew of a Christian orphanage. Someone led him to an evangelical mission we had visited a few months earlier during a brief vacation.

"Is there anyone here working with street kids?" he asked, getting a little nervous.

"No, not here in São Paulo," was the response.

Jonathan's face fell.

"But in Belo Horizonte there's a small group of people working with street kids. Perhaps you could ask them. They're with Youth With A Mission."

Jonathan didn't think twice but took the first flight to Belo Horizonte. He was running out of time, since he had already booked his return trip.

We just missed him when he arrived at the base; we had left town to take care of our visas. But Jonathan knew what he was looking for, and after Jim described the ministry we had started downtown and told him about our plans, he quickly made up his mind, even though he had not met us personally.

"That's it!" he said and told Jim we should go ahead and rent a place in town. He would take care of the rent for the first six months. Then he said, "Good day, mate," and was gone.

Amazed, we listened to Jim after we got home. It sounded so incredible—the Lord using someone from the other side of the world to help us pay rent on a home for street children! One thing was clear, however: it was very important to God that those street children receive help and hear about His love for them.

Greatly encouraged, we began to hunt for a suitable building. It wasn't easy. We needed a home for our family and the eight coworkers we had acquired. The house also had to be large enough to accommodate the street children. It couldn't be too far from downtown but would preferably be on the perimeter. Most landlords weren't too crazy about the idea. They preferred to rent their property to a quiet family or as office space. Every day we prayed about it. Finally, we found something: a house with four bedrooms, a large kitchen, and two bathrooms. In the back was a tiny house, built for servants, with a small bedroom, living room, and kitchen inside and a bathroom outside. Underneath the main house was a large garage we could use as a craft and game room.

The little house in the back looked horrible. Every wall was painted a different color—hot pink, grassy green, light blue, and dark yellow, all of which clashed terribly. Mismatched tiles, probably leftovers from a variety of other jobs, covered the floor. However, the overall space, although somewhat small for our family, would do. An advantage was that the landlord couldn't care less what we used the building for, as long as we paid the rent on time. Another advantage was the location—a side street of the Rua Bonfim, close to our infamous bar. We decided to take it and named it *Casa Resgate* (Rescue House).

Some of our male helpers moved in right away. Our family had to wait three months while we were taking the leadership course at the base. Friends from back home had sent a large gift for a secondhand Volkswagen van. Every day at noon, right after morning classes, Johan would drive to Rescue House to have a meal with the children and work on the house.

Brazilian driving is vastly different from what I was used to. It is so much more aggressive. The rule giving the right of way to vehicles on the right doesn't apply in Brazil. The right of way there means either the larger vehicle (bus or truck), the fastest vehicle, or the most aggressive driver. Anyone waiting his turn has a long wait ahead of him. Even in the busy downtown area many people drive forty miles an hour. Pedestrians never walk across the street; they run, even when they have a green light. Three cars drive abreast in two lanes.

To Johan, this was a challenge, which he quickly mastered. People at the base observed that he was driving like a Brazilian. What took the bus an hour, he could cover in twenty-five minutes! I was always scared when I rode with him and in a constant panic mode, even though Johan patiently explained that if he drove any slower, all the traffic behind him would crash into his bumper. I hated the thought of driving into town myself and postponed it as long as possible. But Pieter and Dilma were now going to school downtown, and soon it would be my turn to drive them to and from school. With sweaty palms I slipped behind the wheel one day, praying the whole way and driving slower than Johan ever had. Thankfully, no one ran into my bumper.

One evening Johan had just returned from downtown. "Jeannette, we met a girl today who was raped last night by a gang of twelve." He looked serious.

We had heard stories about street girls being raped. These girls often became the steady girlfriend of one of the gang leaders. For every wrong move, the slightest misunderstanding, a fight, or any offense, the gang leader would order all other gang members to rape the girl while others kept her down. They called this appalling practice "to be put in a circle."

The two of us were sitting in the kitchen. The children had been asleep for hours.

"Her name is Sonia," Johan continued. "We couldn't do much for her. Not even take her into the new Rescue House." He was right, since only guys were living there. "So we had to let her go back to the streets. It broke my heart."

If we had lived in town we could have taken her in, but the leadership course still had two months to go.

"Could we keep her here until we move? She could sleep in the kitchen," I said, hesitating.

"Mmm, that may not work out either," Johan remarked. "We're both in class in the morning, and who would watch her? I'm always gone in the afternoon, and you would be alone with our own children and her as well. I don't know. Let's pray about it."

We both prayed for Sonia but went to sleep without coming to a decision. The next afternoon Johan called me from town. I could hardly believe what I heard.

"Jeannette, Sonia came by Rescue House this morning. She was bleeding a lot and had been raped again by all the gang members. We took her to the hospital, where the doctor stitched her up, but then he discharged her to us. What do we do now?"

I felt nauseated and realized what a wonderful and protective childhood I had had! I couldn't fathom the depth of depravity of these children and what horrendous things they did to each other.

"Bring her home to the base or else they'll kill her," I said.

"Yeah, I thought so too. See you later." With a deep sigh I hung up the phone.

That night Sonia shyly followed Johan into our home. She was clearly uncomfortable and kept staring at the ground. She looked about fourteen (although we soon found out she was sixteen) and was dressed in one of our coworkers' clothes.

"Hi, Sonia. I am Jeannette. Please come in and join us at the table. We waited for you for supper." I tried to put her at ease. The other children watched her curiously.

After some awkward moments, we ate our first meal together. Sonia hardly said a word, and I think she was glad she could go to sleep right after dinner. We fixed a bed for her on the bench in the kitchen, and soon she was sound asleep.

FIFTEEN

Dilma's Healing

THE next day I gave Sonia some clothes other staff had given us. She beamed and immediately tried everything on. The clothes were far more modest than her own outfits—supershort miniskirts and minuscule T-shirts—had been, but she was genuinely pleased with her new wardrobe.

It took a few days for Sonia to relax and tell us a little about her past. She recalled that when she was just three years old, her parents had pushed her out on the streets to sell roses, individually wrapped in cellophane, to young, amorous couples. She had always been shy and hated the job. When she was four, her dad was put in jail. She had no idea why, but the consequences for her were disastrous. Her mother left her with an aunt who, that same day, dropped her off on a corner of the street in the downtown area. Sonia wasn't familiar with that part of town, didn't know anyone, and couldn't find her way home. She wandered about without food or drink for most of the day, when a police officer picked her up and took her to an orphanage managed by a nun. She stayed there until the nun died when Sonia was twelve.

All seventy-two children from that home were then transferred to FEBEM, a huge government-run orphanage housed in a large, ugly concrete structure where eight hundred children lived. It was more of a correctional facility than an orphanage. The day Sonia arrived, the other girls stole all her clothing and personal items while she was taking a shower. She hated the place and soon plotted with a friend to escape. That was easy. They scaled a fence, took some items from a neighbor's clothesline, and disappeared in the downtown slums. Soon they joined a gang, and Sonia's girlfriend became the "woman" of the gang leader. For the next four years this gave Sonia a measure of protection. That is, until the day before yesterday.

That day her eyes were opened to the extreme cruelty of street children. A fight had erupted among the gang members, and the leader felt it was Sonia's fault and she needed to be taught a lesson. He ordered all the gang members that evening to "put Sonia in the circle." Sonia was helpless against so many of them, and they raped her all night. When they saw her back on the street the next evening and noticed that she was still able to walk normally, the gang leader's fury knew no bounds. They dragged her into a dark alley and repeated her "punishment."

Lord, I prayed silently, *in Your love and mercy, would You please begin to heal these deep emotional wounds in her young life?*

I wasn't sure what to say to her. I had had such a sheltered childhood myself that I couldn't begin to imagine what she had gone through. Nevertheless, I knew the Lord loved her and had known her even in her mother's womb. I knew this had not been His plan for her life, because His plans are always for good. However, our sins and the sins of the people around us can ruin God's plans. I knew Sonia had raw emotional scars, and I didn't want to say anything that sounded shallow. Faltering at first, I began to explain that the Lord Jesus Christ loved her and had died for her. To my delight, she listened intently and immediately began to read the New Testament I had given her. The Bible ministered to her, and for days she devoured it. We prayed together every day, and slowly she began to relax and lose some of her shyness.

Our schedule was stretched to the breaking point, with Sonia at home, Johan going to town in the afternoon, plus the leadership classes, which involved a lot of homework, but we were glad we were able to combine it all. Besides, it was for only a couple of months, at which point the course would be over and we would move to the city.

"DID you hear that Kalafi Moala is going to teach?"

We met Jim outside the large dining room. Kalafi was the Asia YWAM director, and we had heard a lot about him. But what came next was new for us.

"Recently, Kalafi spoke at a church where fifteen deaf people were healed!"

Dubious, we looked at Jim. Old wounds began to resurface.

"No, really! It's true. Apparently, the Lord has used him in similar healings. Wouldn't it be wonderful if he could pray for Dilma?" Jim said expectantly.

"Yes, perhaps…," Johan hesitated.

Surprised at our lack of enthusiasm, Jim raised one eyebrow.

"I really would ask him if I were you!" he called as he walked off.

Silently we stared at each other; then, deep in thought, Johan and I slowly strolled to our little home. I suddenly realized that the roots of my deep pain were still there and wondered whether Johan felt the same. It was a topic we had never discussed. I decided to take a walk and talk it over with the Lord.

Lord, is this really what You want? Are You going to heal Dilma?

I began to cry.

Are You going to use a YWAM leader? Is that why You waited?

Many questions crowded my mind.

Lord, why am I crying? Why am I so disappointed when I know You care about us so deeply?

Ashamed, I kept on walking. The steep path from the base led to a winding trail hemmed in by thick shrubbery and trees. I knew I could unburden myself here—no one would find me. It seemed as though I was suddenly carrying an unbearable load. Drained and exhausted, I sank down on a fallen tree trunk. Tears now streamed freely down my face.

Lord, I don't dare hope again for healing. What if it doesn't happen?

I felt the intense burden of coping with raising a daughter with a disability. It hurt far more than I had expected it would. I was also angry with myself. Where was my faith in the Lord? What kind of missionary was I, telling others to rely on God when I didn't have the nerve to do so myself? I, Jeannette, who didn't want to go through that lonely sense of abandonment again if God decided not to answer my prayers.

I perched on that tree trunk for a long time and felt strangely relieved after unburdening my soul to God. I had expected God to be deeply disappointed with my doubts, but instead I had the distinct feeling that He understood perfectly and wanted to comfort me. My heart finally settled down.

All right, Lord, I was able to pray, *Your will be done.*

I was still hoping that Dilma would be healed. I still believed that God could do it, but I never wanted to doubt His love again, either for Dilma or for us, even if she were to remain deaf her whole life. Though I didn't understand it, I wanted to leave this matter with Him, as He always has our best interest at heart. Slowly, the hope that had almost died within me began to bloom again. I walked home and told Johan everything that night. He understood perfectly, because God was taking us both along the same path.

Kalafi arrived and was teaching that week. He immediately agreed to pray for Dilma during the next service. I was still anxious.

"Lord, it doesn't matter what happens," I whispered as Kalafi called us to the front. "I know You love us and I love You."

Kalafi was a friendly, quiet man who took his time shaking our hands. He then placed Dilma in front of him. Dilma focused her large brown eyes on his face as he gently put his hands on her head. The hall became quiet. We were surrounded by over a hundred people, most of them YWAM staff who all knew Dilma and her past—people who believed in God and trusted that He would heal her. The air became laden with expectancy.

Kalafi began to pray softly. After one or two sentences, he suddenly stopped. It seemed as though he was listening. For a moment he was silent; then he began to pray for a healing of her inner wounds. How did he know that?

He prayed that God would erase painful memories. In my mind I suddenly saw that old cardboard box she had lived in for so long and realized that the way her parents had treated her had left far larger wounds than her deafness ever would.

"Please, Lord," I prayed along, full of faith, "heal her from all those awful memories that left such deep wounds in her heart."

Instantly I had the assurance that this was what God wanted to do. I realized how much Dilma's abandonment and suffering had grieved Him and that He, as a loving Father, wanted to shield and protect her. That was one of the main reasons Robson's team had found her in that box: God wanted to heal her mind. A deep peace welled up inside me.

"Amen," Kalafi said.

"Amen," I heard tens of others repeat behind me. I squeezed Johan's hand. He gave me a smile and grabbed Dilma's hand. I still didn't understand: Dilma's hearing had not been restored, but I was no longer disappointed. On the contrary, I was ecstatic and believed with all my heart that God had done something very special in Dilma.

Grateful, I tucked the children in bed that night.

"Did God heal Dilma, Mom?" Pieter piped up from under his blanket.

"Yes," I whispered softly in his ear, "God did heal her but not her hearing."

Surprised, he turned to me.

"Then what did He heal in her?"

"It's kind of hard to see, but God healed some very sore spots in her heart."

I was at a loss how to explain it more fully. The next day Dilma herself explained it. From one day to the other her behavior changed. She was much easier to get along with. If before she was hyperactive, disobedient, and easily frustrated, now she seemed to quietly absorb everything around her, was more respectful, and was easier to handle.

This change continued, and it became obvious that she wasn't as unsure of herself as before. Earlier, her school supervisor had told me that her teacher had almost had a nervous breakdown because of Dilma's behavior, but now they, too, saw a marked change in Dilma.

God was with us. With renewed hope and energy, we concentrated on the ministry ahead of us: our mission to help street kids.

SIXTEEN

Worries

BEFORE we had started our work with street children, several people had warned us: "Watch out for those children—you can't trust them. They have weapons, and they'll kill for a dime." It was true that most of them carried knives. The first day that we opened Rescue House, we had caught several children trying to steal silverware. By the second day we decided not to give them any knives with their meals. A few days later we were amazed that they could even make a dangerous weapon from a fork by removing the teeth and then scraping the ends on the rough sidewalk surface until they became as sharp as needle points. That's when we switched to plastic.

We also met children who had killed people. Usually they did this during a fight with other street children, and they were often under the influence of drugs or glue at the time.

It didn't take the children long to realize that they were not to take items to Rescue House. That simply was not allowed. As a result, many of the kids had secret hiding places on the street—space behind a loose tile or the grate of a gutter—where they kept their treasures such as knives and other weapons. They also stashed their stolen goods—watches, gold chains, and the like—in those spaces until they could find a convenient time to pawn them.

In spite of our discipline, occasional fights still erupted at Rescue House. These fights could quickly escalate unless our workers intervened and separated the parties involved. The kitchen became a dangerous area. Every morning the staff prepared sixty to ninety meals. Of these, thirty were packaged in disposable containers to be distributed on the streets, while the other kids and staff ate theirs in the dining room. It was always a scramble to get everything done in time, and the staff could not keep track of all the kitchen knives or keep all the children out of the kitchen area. On one occasion during a fight, knives came whizzing through the air. Two girls had gotten into an argument. They ran to the kitchen, opened a drawer, took some knives, and tried to stab each other. Thankfully, they had poor aim, but our workers were pretty shaken up.

Rescue House had been open for a month. None of the staff had had any experience with these children before, but they all learned fast. Johan seemed to have a special gift for dealing with this type of children. At first the staff needed him to intervene in every fight to separate the fighters, calm them down, and see that they didn't resume fighting as soon as he turned his back. Sometimes it was quite dangerous for him to separate two children, especially if they used knives or broken pieces of sharp glass, but so far he had been successful.

But one rainy evening I became concerned. It was eight o'clock, and Johan still wasn't home. We had twelve coworkers by now. The guys, all single and in their early twenties, lived at Rescue House. The girls took the bus into town every day and returned to the base with Johan in the van. The guys were usually home by seven. But now they still weren't home. They never came home this late! If something had happened, they could have called me.

The children had gone to bed, and Sonia was on the couch crocheting a pink scarf. I had just that afternoon taught her how to do this, and she was totally engrossed in her work, holding the hook close to her face. She had been living with us for several weeks, and all was going well. In the morning when we were in class, she helped out at the house under the supervision of another staff member. In the afternoon I did a Bible study with her, and she helped with cooking, the laundry, and the care of the children. She was a nice girl, but I still didn't trust her enough to let her be alone with our children. I couldn't quite explain to Johan why I felt this way—perhaps I was just an overprotective mother.

An hour went slowly by. I stood up to make another pot of tea. It was pitch black outside and raining hard. The rain turned into a tropical storm with huge lightning flashes and loud thunder, but since this was the rainy season, no one was alarmed. Storms like this often happened every few days. The fact that our electricity went out for several hours during each storm wasn't anything new either. Our home had candles everywhere, and usually they created an intimate atmosphere. But this time I did not appreciate those little dancing flames. I shivered and felt more and more apprehensive.

Why aren't they here yet? Are they in trouble with the street kids?

I carefully carried two mugs with piping-hot tea to the living room. Sonia was putting away her things, getting ready for bed. Once again I looked at my watch. I was too anxious to crochet or read, so after I prayed with Sonia I decided to go to bed as well. The hands on the clock crawled toward ten. Outside, the downpour continued uninterrupted. The sheets of rain hitting the window irritated me.

What if Johan has been in an accident or was stabbed by a street kid?

During the entire evening I had tried to suppress thoughts of both those possibilities, but now they had resurfaced. I tried to think of something else to ease my mind. I told myself to quit being stupid, but it was too late for that. I recalled one of our workers telling me recently that he had heard a big kid high on drugs threatening Johan, saying he was going to kill him. Threats like that didn't seem to faze Johan.

"Of course we're going to hit some resistance," he had warned us many times. "Why not? Up until now the streets had belonged to the devil, and he had managed to destroy a lot of lives. By trying to rescue these children we've created a war zone, so there's going to be fierce opposition."

I was sitting on the edge of my bed.

Lord, You wouldn't allow that to happen now, would You? You know we're here to serve You.

I suddenly recalled how I naively assumed that the Lord would always protect us from problems because He needed us. I had been devastated when the popular Christian singer Keith Green and his two oldest children were killed in a plane crash. Three weeks earlier Keith had given a concert on the *Anastasis.* He had given lots of concerts and was doing a great work for the Lord. Hundreds of young people had given their lives to the Lord because of his ministry and testimony. He was only twenty-eight years old when he died. His wife, Melody, was pregnant at the time, and I admired her deep faith. She wasn't bitter, and although she didn't understand, she chose to keep her trust and faith in the Lord. I had read several of her newsletters and was always amazed at her strength. God helped her through this most difficult time. But God wouldn't ask that of me now, would He? He knew that Johan was indispensable in reaching these street kids for Him. He knew that we had four small children. He knew…

Suddenly I heard the still, small voice of the Lord: *Jeannette, who do you love more, Johan or Me?*

Lord! I didn't dare answer that question. I fell on my knees next to the bed, tears flooding my eyes. A leadlike heaviness pressed in on me. It seemed like eternity before I was able to whisper, "Lord, I want to love You the most. I am very grateful for Johan, but I know You need to be number one in my life."

The voice persisted. *Do you want to follow Me no matter what?*

I was caught up in a huge battle.

Lord, Johan belongs to You—he doesn't belong to me. I know that. I would love to keep him here, but if You want to call Him home…that's okay too. I want to trust You.

I don't remember how long it took me to honestly say these words. I was chilled to the bone and stiff from kneeling on that cold, damp floor, but I had peace in my heart. I didn't know what the future would hold, but I knew that God was with me. I picked up my flashlight and looked at my watch. It was eleven-thirty.

I heard a car suddenly drive up to the parking area behind our home. I scrambled for my rain boots and ran outside. It was still raining, but I didn't care. Johan had come home with the rest of the team. I was so grateful.

"What happened? Why are you so late?"

Johan hopped out of the car.

"We had car trouble, and it took forever to fix it. We couldn't call because of the blackout. All the phone lines were down."

Surprised, I stopped in my tracks. Such a simple explanation. I could have figured that out myself. All this panic for nothing?

No, it wasn't for nothing. I knew that God had used this situation to test me. He wanted to get me through this to teach me something. I was actually grateful now for those scary hours but also immensely happy to see Johan and our team alive and well standing before me.

I ran inside to fix hot chocolate for everyone.

SEVENTEEN

Michele Is Missing!

AT FIRST all had gone well with Sonia, but now problems were beginning to develop. A few times we caught her smoking. When I asked her where she got the cigarettes, she said a man in a bar about a mile from the base had given them to her. I was surprised she even knew there was a bar in the area and decided to keep a closer eye on her.

Things began to disappear from my kitchen cabinets. Cookies and candy were missing. Then a full jar of jam was suddenly empty. One day, thirty minutes after I had taken it from the oven, half a cake vanished. I had spoken to Sonia several times about stealing, and we had looked up Bible verses about not stealing, but nothing seemed to make any difference.

"Sonia, do you remember Leo?"

Leo was a street kid we had known for some time.

"Yes, why?"

"Did you know that just a few weeks before you came to live here he went into foster care at the home of a jeweler?"

"No, I didn't know that. Does he like it there?"

"He *did* like it," I corrected her. "They were very good to him, and in the afternoon they even let him help in the store. The jeweler planned to train him in the business. He learned a lot and did very well. He was serving customers and selling a lot of merchandise. The jeweler had one watch Leo wasn't supposed to touch. It was an antique heirloom and worth a lot of money. It was displayed in the window just as an ornament. The jeweler would never sell it and told Leo several times never to touch that watch."

Sonia was all ears.

"A few days ago, Leo had an urge to sniff some glue and hang out with the old street gang. He knew he shouldn't do this anymore, but he kept thinking about it anyway. Then when the jeweler went out on an errand, Leo was left alone for five minutes. The temptation was too strong for him. He grabbed that special watch, worth thousands of *cruzeiros,* and ran to the *favela.*

Sonia's eyes widened.

"He found the guy who used to buy his stolen stuff and sold it for thirty *cruzeiros.*"

"How stupid!" Sonia blurted. She looked angry.

It seemed I was getting through to her and she was beginning to see how wrong it was to steal.

"Yes," I agreed, "it was stupid. The shopkeeper fired Leo and told him never to come back. Leo's future was ruined."

"How stupid! How stupid!" Sonia repeated.

I was glad she understood.

Then, banging her fist on the table, she screamed, "He could have sold it for much more!"

Things got worse by the day. Not only did Sonia steal; she also lied and refused to listen to us. This created a difficult situation in our home. Once in a while she would still play with the children, especially Michele, who was almost a year old and delighted when Sonia spent time with her. I wasn't too crazy about that and tried to keep them both in my sight.

One Saturday afternoon Sonia disappeared, and Michele was gone too. Nobody had seen them. I became panicky and recalled stories about homeless girls who lived on the streets with their babies. Most of these babies didn't make it. The mothers themselves were still children with no sense of responsibility, nor did they know how to care for those babies. Sometimes they would cling to the back of a moving bus, high on drugs, while holding their baby by an arm or a leg. They fed their babies drugs, and often the various gangs would try out new drugs on the babies. Recently, an eighteen-month-old had been admitted to an intensive care unit after a street kid tried to rape her.

I immediately warned Johan, who turned white, grabbed our car keys, and ran off yelling, "I'll try to catch up with the bus to town."

If Sonia had taken the bus into town, Johan had a small chance of catching her before they reached the downtown area. Several people had heard about the incident and had started a prayer vigil. I was too upset to think rationally, and I allowed ugly thoughts to erupt: *Don't you see? It's too hard to get these kids off the streets. Your own family suffers. You're crazy to put your life and that of your kids in danger.*

Angrily I pushed back these thoughts. I knew they were lies! The Lord had brought us here. He knew we had children, and He loved them as much as He loved the street children. The hours passed very slowly.

Suddenly someone yelled, "Jeannette! Look! There they are! Down the hill, behind those bushes."

I ran down the hill. Panting, I grabbed Michele from Sonia's arms. Sonia looked at me with surprise. No, she hadn't planned to run away at all; she had just gone for a walk. I hugged Michele tightly, then stared at Sonia. I knew I couldn't trust her again; there had been too many lies the past few days. We walked back home in silence, arriving just as Johan returned. With tears in his eyes, he took Michele from me.

I was dead tired and suddenly realized my body was still shaking. I wanted to remain calm in front of the children and not let them know how deeply shocked we were, but it wasn't easy. I needed to be alone and decided to take a shower. The hot water felt good, and slowly I began to relax, but this released such a flood of pent-up emotions that I had to throw up. Never before had I been this upset.

Lord, what are we to do?

Sonia looked at me timidly when, after quite a while, I walked back into the room. Johan had spoken firmly to her, but she had looked at him with vacant eyes. He shrugged his shoulders when he saw me. I didn't know what to say to her either. I was still too upset about what could have happened.

We all went to bed early that night.

"Are you sure it's not going to be too dangerous?" I whispered. Johan was tossing next to me, and I knew he too was concerned.

"The Lord called us to Brazil, right? And God told us to work with street children."

"I'm listening."

Johan stared at the ceiling, then continued, "God knows we have children. He gave them to us. I believe He'll take care of us."

I believed that too, but where was the boundary between faith and taking irresponsible risks for yourself and your children? We knew lots of people who felt we had already gone too far. I had read many books about missionaries who had gone to difficult and faraway countries over the past centuries. Many had buried their children at a young age, as their little bodies had no resistance against tropical diseases. Some of those mothers, like Dorothy Carey, never got over these sad events. Others received renewed strength from God and the power to continue to spread the gospel in spite of their heavy personal losses.

How dangerous was this kind of life going to be for our children? Would they make friends with the street children and then take on their bad habits, or would they be an example to them? Would our children be grateful later on in life that they had grown up as missionary children, or would they be resentful that they had missed out on a "normal" childhood? Would our lifestyle bring our children closer to God and cause them to love Him more, or would the price be too high and turn them away from Him in rebellion?

We had planned to move our family soon to those ugly little servant quarters behind Rescue House. How was that going to work out for our children? The small building had only one bedroom for all five of them. We would put a mattress on the floor in the tiny living room at night for us to sleep on. The roof and the ceiling were full of holes through which blew a steady stream of brown dust, that is, when it didn't rain. But that wasn't the worst. The worst was the tiny inside patio that would be the children's only playground. Here at the base they were used to the wide-open spaces. I wondered how in the world I could keep four active children occupied all day in that small space. And wouldn't they miss all their friends from the orphanage? Johan and I talked for a long time.

"Hasn't the Lord guided us step-by-step?" Johan asked. "Let's pray about it." We held hands and told God about all our worries and misgivings. It was a great release, and I felt the tension of this day finally beginning to lift.

Lord, will You please shelter our kids when we move to town? I prayed, *and will You help us make this fun for them so they'll be looking forward to the move?*

I KNEW how easily children pick up on our moods, so I tried to hide my apprehension. We remained upbeat about the upcoming move and reiterated its advantages: we would live close to our work, see Daddy more often, and not have to drive so far to take Dilma and Pieter to school. Pieter had just enrolled at a huge elementary school with about seven thousand students, and Dilma attended a school for the deaf. I was desperately trying to see this whole adventure in a positive light and asked God to help the children and us with this big move. Even though it costs us something to follow the Lord, the rewards are great. It's so wonderful to know Him and feel the peace of obedience. I hoped our children would learn this as well.

I had no idea how the Lord was going to answer our prayer requests, but that same week God showed us His incredible love, not just for Johan and me, but especially for our children.

"I would like you to use this money to get something fun for the children, like a plastic swimming pool." Surprised, I stared at the note folded around a check in my hand. It had come from a good friend back in the Netherlands. What a great idea! A swimming pool! Why hadn't we thought of that? About ten months out of the year we had great, sunny weather in Brazil, ideal for a little swimming pool. If it wasn't too big, it would just fit the seven-by-ten-foot patio space between the big house and our little place. Excited, I showed the note to Johan and the children. Everyone's face lit up!

"When are we going to get it, Mom? When are we going to move? When can we swim?"

Within a week one of our prayers had been answered: our children were looking forward to the move and could hardly wait to move into their new home with the swimming pool. We were very grateful.

A few days later Sonia ran away.

EIGHTEEN

A Whole Gang Gets off the Street

O N E night when I was going to sign language class, I noticed a crowd at the curb of a busy shopping area. It was twilight, which in Brazil means it would be completely dark in half an hour. When I came closer, I saw a couple of police officers and a bunch of children. Two of the larger boys were being handcuffed. I guessed their ages at younger than sixteen. Some of the smaller boys, grimy kids in torn T-shirts and shorts, watched nearby. Most of them were barefooted. Passersby watched from a distance. Curious, I moved closer to get a better look. After all, these were street children, the very reason we had come to Brazil. Somehow I felt responsible and pushed my way to the front.

"What's going on?" I addressed the officer closest to me who had a firm grip on the arm of one of the boys. The officer turned and looked me up and down.

"Nothing is going on, lady; please move along."

But I wasn't about to be intimidated.

"Where are you taking these children, and what have they done?" Other curious pedestrians stopped and listened. The officer pushed the boy impatiently toward the gray police cruiser parked at the curb. The boy did not resist and held his head down. For a moment he looked at me, and I saw tears in his eyes. He was skinny, with light brown, curly hair and fair skin. The other boy the police were arresting was just the opposite. His face was black, round, and angry, and he violently resisted. The officer slapped him several times, and expletives I was as yet unfamiliar with crackled through the putrid air.

"These guys were sniffing glue, and we'll teach them a lesson at the precinct."

He pushed the boy roughly along. The onlookers stepped back to make way. The smaller children gazed at me expectantly. With sudden courage I took a few steps forward and blocked them.

"I'd like to take these boys and be responsible for them." I tried to speak with authority but was just as surprised at my own audacity as the police officers and the children were.

"But, ma'am, these children are very dangerous. What are you going to do with them?"

The sad face of the quiet boy lit up with a glimmer of hope. The smaller children crowded around us.

"We have a home for these children. It's called Rescue House, and we want to help them." Actually, we had only day-care facilities, since we didn't yet have a permit for keeping anyone overnight, but I felt that this was an emergency that called for an exception.

The officer laughed in derision.

"Lady, we are the only ones who can solve this problem." With one hand he pushed the quiet boy against the gray patrol car. With the other hand he opened the door. The other officer had his hands full with the wild boy who fought him every step of the way.

I turned to the quiet boy.

"What's your name?"

"Marcos," he answered softly.

"Marcos, we want to help you. As soon as they let you go, would you come to visit us?"

The impatient police officer pushed Marcos next to his friend in the backseat of the car. He slammed the door shut, jumped in front, and turned the key in the ignition. As the car screeched away, I yelled our address to Marcos. He looked at me with large, moist eyes, but I wasn't sure he understood. The sirens shrieked through the night air but were quickly drowned out at the next crossing by protesting drivers demanding the right of way.

I felt so helpless. The pedestrians dispersed, and the children, when they realized the police officers were serious about arresting their leaders, quickly vanished. The street returned to its usual scene of hurried pedestrians and honking cars as though nothing had happened. But two teenagers had been arrested. I couldn't get that picture out of my mind. When I got home that night I was outraged and related the whole incident to Johan. Little did we know that this first brief contact with Marcos would have life-changing consequences.

Two days later Johan reported, "Jeannette, guess who came to Rescue House today? Marcos, his friend Jabu, and their whole gang."

So Marcos had heard me correctly after all! When the police released them two days later, the boys found their gang members, and the next morning, bright and early, they were waiting at our door. Marcos had difficulty walking. His toes had been beaten with a bat until they were black and blue, but he was glad that that was all they did to him. The police often used far worse tactics, such as the so-called parrot stick, a notorious torture instrument. The children were hung on this stick by their knees, then beaten.

Marcos and Jabu's gang consisted of fifteen boys between the ages of six and sixteen. Our team members had talked to all of them privately and asked why they were living on the street. Their stories were similar. Often the children gravitated to the streets because their parents were poor, or they lived in the slums and their parents drank a lot. Frequently, their fathers had deserted them and they didn't get along with their stepfathers. They were often ordered to go to the streets to bring home some money. It didn't take them long to figure out that it was much easier not to go home at all and to keep the earned or stolen money themselves.

Initially, living on the street seemed like high adventure—just roaming around all day with other children, with no responsibilities and no orders to follow, and sleeping whenever they felt like it and eating only things they liked. I even once met a girl who lived entirely on Popsicles and ice cream sundaes. For breakfast she stole Popsicles from a freezer of a downtown bakery, and the rest of the day she tried various ways to get money to buy large banana splits.

The children played cops and robbers with real police officers, defying them to catch them and then hiding in alleys. They loved to hang on to the back of a moving bus in shopping areas and scare pedestrians. They found it exciting to go to sleep with a group of other children somewhere in an alley very late at night—almost like summer camp—that is, until they witnessed their first street fight and watched children being brutally injured or even killed; until the police were faster than they figured and arrested them; until they were hungry and cold, got sick, quarreled, or got lonely and afraid. That's when they learned how sniffing that thick, strong glue could dull their anxieties and make them feel strong and courageous.

All of Marcos and Jabu's gang members came from one of the three hundred slums in Belo Horizonte. We carefully recorded their addresses, and the day after they arrived, our staff began to visit their families. We prayed about other ways we could help them.

There was a lot of work to be done, but thankfully our team was growing. We had just received a letter from a Dutch couple, Jan and Sofia, who were eager to come with their two children and help. We looked forward to their arrival and decided they could live at our home at the base until we could find housing for them in town.

Our three-month leadership training course was over, and right after graduating we moved into our tiny house-with-pool behind Rescue House. Our coworkers moved into the main building. In those four small bedrooms at Rescue House we managed to cram thirteen people snugly together. Since the rooms were too small for cupboards, the residents stashed their belongings in a heap at the foot of their bunk beds. Across the room they strung some clotheslines for towels and other items. The front bedroom, where six young women roomed together, soon became known as our *favela*.

NINETEEN

New Strategies

MARCOS and Jabu and their gang showed up every day. Since we still didn't have a permit to house underage children, they came early in the morning, and at night Johan transported them in our van back to their sleeping quarters for the night, usually a large portico at a store entrance.

Every morning at Rescue House the children took a hot shower and put on clean clothes. The dirty clothes were laundered and ready to wear the next day. After a large mug of hot, sweet tea and sandwiches for breakfast, the children moved to the basement, where Johan and a few other creative coworkers kept them busy. One group of children were taught how to use a small handsaw; another group made macramé plant hangers. Many of these children had never or, at best, had only briefly attended school. They were very pleased with themselves when at the end of a day's hard work they had actually made a car, a plane, or a puzzle. Everyone had to admire his or her own creation, and they all grinned from ear to ear. At times they also painted their handiwork and often, during the process, themselves as well.

I had left a few of Pieter and Johanneke's large coloring books in a corner of the workplace, and big fifteen- and sixteen-year-olds would fight over them. These young people had never done anything like it, and it was moving to see their deep concentration as they tried to color within the lines.

At eleven in the morning, Johan had the children put everything away and herded them all to the large living room, where they sat on the floor in a circle. We had no furniture as yet, but nobody cared. Johan kept his audience spellbound as he told them Bible stories.

We also taught the children the latest Portuguese worship songs and performed skits to make the Bible stories come to life. After just two days, Marcos decided to give his life to the Lord Jesus and quit using drugs and stealing. Every day he came back with his entourage and, as their leader, forbade them to steal or do drugs. Since the boys spent most of the day with us and were fed three meals a day, they actually had no need to steal anymore.

Marcos's gang went along with the new rules, and it wasn't long before Jabu and all the other boys also decided to become disciples of the Lord Jesus. Their natural practices, especially their nocturnal ones, changed radically. Marcos, who had lived on the streets since he was eleven, and Jabu, who had lost both parents when he was only seven, had up until then forced their young followers to rip gold necklaces off women's necks as they shopped. The children knew someone in the slums who would take these items in exchange for drugs or glue. The gang obtained food by forcing the younger children to beg or rob the cash register in one of the bars. Usually the children didn't go to sleep until one or two in the morning.

Now they stayed with us all day, and at night, before going to sleep, they all sat together, wrapped in blankets to stay warm, singing worship songs! They didn't become angels overnight, but during the following weeks we noticed tremendous changes. Take Michael, who threw a fit one morning when he discovered that someone had stolen his shoes while he slept. He was livid and threatened to kill the thief if he ever saw him. Johan took him aside and explained the meaning of forgiveness. At first, Michael didn't listen, but after a while Johan got through to him.

"Okay," he said, "so if I see that dude [he knew by now who it was], I'm supposed to forgive him?"

Johan explained that God, who has forgiven us much, expects us to do the same. Michael listened quietly.

"How are you going to forgive him, Michael?" Johan asked him.

A short silence followed. Suddenly, a huge grin spread over his face.

"I know what I'll do," he declared. "I'll shake his hand and tell him God loves him and forgave him."

Immediately, Michael jumped up and left to carry out his mission. A few hours later he returned wearing his shoes. It turned out that the thief had been so blown away by Michael's behavior that he returned the stolen shoes at once.

While some of our workers were involved in the immediate care of these children at Rescue House, others were busy visiting the parents of Marcos and Jabu's gang members. They located several families who said they would like to have their children back, and seven young boys were reunited with their parents. The boys continued to receive assistance and counseling, which often took months or, for some, years.

Wanderley was one of those boys. After he had been visiting our home for a few weeks, he came down with a severe case of the flu. His fever was so high we didn't dare take him back to the street that night. He stayed with us, but the next day his condition was worse. I decided to take him to the doctor, who diagnosed pneumonia and a serious liver condition.

"If this boy isn't hospitalized and treated, he'll be dead in a few days," the doctor gravely announced. I froze. Now what?

Getting someone admitted to a hospital in Brazil is quite a challenge. Some patients drive from one hospital to another to find an empty bed. Many times the patient dies before a space is found. That whole afternoon we tried one hospital after another without any luck. Then we finally did find a bed, but the hospital wouldn't admit Wanderley because he was a street kid and had no papers or ID.

"We need a signature from his parents before we can admit him," the admittance clerk told us.

"His parents have moved," I explained, "and one of our staff is trying to find them."

"Well, why don't you come back after you find them?"

"Wanderley hasn't had any contact with his parents for months, he is critically ill, and we can't wait," I pleaded. "Can't you admit him without a signature?"

"No, ma'am. Rules are rules."

I said a quick silent prayer.

"Can't I sign for him?"

The admittance clerk gave me a surprised look.

"Do you want to be responsible for a street kid?" Her shrill voice echoed through the halls. Wanderley, next to me, watched in silence.

I had no idea what this responsibility included, but I knew that God had called me to Brazil to take care of street children and this kid was going to die if he didn't get some medical help.

"Of course," I said and picked up the pen from the counter. "No problem."

The woman, still incredulous, produced a stack of forms for me to sign. I signed everything without reading any of it. My knowledge of Portuguese was not sufficient to understand all those terms anyway. I just hoped that I wasn't getting myself into a heap of trouble.

After an IV and antibiotics were started, Wanderley quickly improved. Everyone had prayed for him. We were pleased when Niceu, a coworker, finally located Wanderley's parents. For a while now, they had regretted their decision to send their son to the streets, especially when they had heard that he was on drugs. Niceu explained the gospel to them, and they both were ready for a new start in life. They asked the Lord to forgive them, and a few days later when they visited Wanderley in the hospital, they asked for his forgiveness as well. Wanderley got well so fast that he was discharged a few days later and could celebrate Christmas with his parents at home.

WE HAD been extremely busy with Christmas preparations. The street children needed to know that the Lord Jesus was vital in our lives and that celebrating His birth was a most significant event. To the daily fare of rice and beans we added six huge, golden brown, roasted turkeys, mountains of French fries, and a cake covering half the table-top that boldly proclaimed, "I love the Lord Jesus!"

I had baked most of that cake in several layers the evening before in our little house in back of Rescue House and had to use eight large cake pans. After putting the last batch in the oven in our tiny kitchen, I fell into bed around eleven. We had also baked sixteen hundred cookies to be stuffed into bags and distributed to two hundred street children. I couldn't look at another cookie, and I promptly forgot about the cake in the oven. When I woke up at six the next morning, the cake was black and so was the wall behind the oven. I had almost burned the house down! Half an hour later, frightened but grateful that nothing more serious had happened, I shoved another cake pan into the oven and this time took it out on time.

On December 24 at five in the afternoon we were ready for the children to start the celebrations. Of Marcos's gang, only three children were left. Seven had been reunited with their families, one had moved to foster care, and four had gone to an orphanage. The three who were left—Marcos, Jabu, and Elen-Cleber—had moved into Rescue House, as we now had an official permit to house them. We had invited another fifty street children, all of whom showed up. The living room was crammed with noisy, excited youngsters. Each little hand had to touch the plastic Christmas tree with its bright electric lights—something they had never seen up close. Intrigued, they unscrewed and screwed the little lightbulbs and touched the big silver ornaments.

After loud, foot-stomping, clapping renditions of several worship songs, Johan took control of the rowdy bunch and narrated the Christmas story, using hand and body motions to put more meaning to his words. The children were mesmerized. I slipped into the kitchen to help serve Christmas dinner on the long rows of blue plastic plates on the table. Suddenly, a small kid shot by me. He didn't look more than four. Quick as lightning he pulled a drawer open and snatched a knife.

"Hey! What are you doing?" I barely managed to grab his arm before he exited the kitchen. Frightened, he looked at me. "I don't want dinner and I don't want cake. I just want a knife so I can stab people when they pester me at night."

Nothing I said convinced the boy to give up that knife. It turned out the little guy was six, and our staff had seen him before. He went by the nickname of Mickey Mouse because of his large ears. I was shocked when I realized he wasn't impressed with the party and wasn't looking forward to Christmas dinner. The presents, new clothes, and a plastic car wrapped in bright red paper waiting for him in a huge basket didn't interest him either. It was clear that this child was no longer a child. He had been robbed of his childhood and didn't know the longings, the dreams, the games, and the hopes of a child. His only concern was to defend his life.

With tears in my eyes, I pried back his tiny fingers, still clenched tightly around the sharp, pointed knife. Frustrated, he tried to kick me. Then he ran out of the kitchen, through the hallway, and out the front door, where he disappeared into the night. I felt totally helpless and intensely sad.

The festivities continued until late at night. Early the next morning most of the boys were back and joined our staff back on the streets. We divided into groups of five to ten and went downtown looking for other street children. We took disposable food containers with Christmas dinners, bags filled with cookies, stickers, and comic books about Christmas. We planned to eat Christmas dinner with the street children on their own turf. That idea proved to be a winner, and all our teams were welcomed with open arms.

Our own group discovered a family under a railroad overpass. Their home consisted of a few yards of soggy soil cordoned off by some large boxes. In one of these we spotted a few empty cans. That was their kitchen. A dilapidated cooking pot sat on a few blackened bricks. The pot was empty. In a corner was a dirty, thin single mattress covered with a torn blanket.

The husband was friendly and shook our hands. When he heard that we were coming to dine with his family he gave us a broad, toothless smile. The woman was very pregnant and surrounded by several dirty, poorly dressed children. They stood in a circle around us, then offered some old boxes to sit on. Our own children were a little timid at first, but after seeing a boxful of puppies and kittens, their fear was soon forgotten. We narrated the Christmas story and had everyone's attention.

"Before we eat we would like to pray for you. Would that be all right?"

We had no idea how they would react. This was the first time we celebrated Christmas with total strangers under a bridge, near roaring traffic. What would they think? We were pleasantly surprised at their openness and hospitality, and they gave us a list of things they would like prayer for. They respectfully closed their eyes; even the children got quiet. To talk to God about their needs was a whole new experience. As a train thundered overhead and buses and cars sped by, we felt God's peace and love for these street people. Afterward, everyone devoured a dinner of rice, beans, and turkey.

All the teams came home that day with exciting stories. Many had dreaded not being able to celebrate Christmas at home with their own families, but now they were glad they had stayed and spent this Christmas in Brazil so they could give to others. We believed the Lord Jesus was pleased too.

By this time Rescue House had become well known among the street children, and we didn't have to venture out in our van to find them. Bright and early every morning they showed up. One of the boys who demanded much of our time was Jorge, a very active thirteen-year-old who couldn't sit still. He came from a small town about a four-hour bus ride from Belo Horizonte. When he was only seven, he had left home for the streets, urged along by older friends and neighborhood children. He soon became the leader of the smaller children in his gang. When it came to painting and other crafts at Rescue House, he was three times as fast as anyone else. However, his projects were always messy, and he broke quite a few tools. He found it very difficult to spend the entire day in the confines of Rescue House, which originally had been built as a one-family home. He was addicted to the open spaces on the streets, where he could do whatever he pleased.

Frustrated, he stomped off several times, sometimes even before we had eaten. Yet he always returned, and one day he surprised us by announcing that God had called him to be a missionary among the Indians in the Amazon region. He was convinced that that was what God wanted him to do. The only problem was that he wasn't willing to surrender his whole life to God. He understood that if he were to become a follower of the Lord Jesus Christ, he could no longer steal, use drugs, or have sex with the street girls, but he was not willing to give up any of these activities. He participated in our Bible studies but decided to stay out on the street.

T H E Dutch TV crew who had filmed us a few months earlier had shown the documentary on national Dutch television. As a result, we received many unexpected responses from viewers. People sent us encouraging notes, prayed for us, or mailed financial support. There were even some viewers who wanted to come and help out with the work. One was a young woman, Carla, who had worked as an X-ray technician in Dordrecht for a couple of years. She had just completed her DTS (Discipleship Training School) in the Netherlands and felt called to help abandoned and rejected children. We gladly accepted her offer. We also acquired Brazilian helpers who had taken the DTS course at the base in Belo Horizonte and then joined the Rescue House staff.

The home was open seven days a week from 9 A.M. until 6 P.M. We all got up at 5:30 to have our quiet time, and at 7:30, after breakfast, we met with the staff for an hour of worship, prayer, and planning for the day. At 8:30 we made assignments for the day, and half an hour later we opened our doors. We welcomed all the children—as many as sixty—one by one, wrote down their names, and listened to feedback before putting them, three at a time, under the shower. Around six in the evening they went back to the street.

Each member of our staff worked very long days. I tried to combine my share of the work with the care of my own children. After six months some of the workers began to show signs of chronic fatigue. Johan, on the other hand, hardly ever got tired. He had an endless supply of energy and seldom took a break. Therefore, it took him a while to realize that our plates were far too full and our schedule had to be revised.

We all felt we should spend more time in prayer with our coworkers and figure out how to best divide our workday. The problem was, we had almost no time to pray together, as every day was completely filled. Eventually we became convinced that to have sufficient time to hear from the Lord, we needed to close shop for a while.

It was hard to tell the street kids to stay away for a couple of days, but we didn't know what else to do. When we started the ministry at Rescue House, we had looked for other people in Brazil who were doing a similar work so that we could learn from them. But we discovered that, even though there were orphanages for poor children, ministries who helped street children were unheard of. So we had to figure it all out by ourselves.

The reason we had kept Rescue House open seven days a week was so that children wouldn't go hungry some days. Now we knew better. The children were not completely dependent on us for food. In addition to serving meals at Rescue House, we provided thirty meals for children on the streets. In spite of this effort, we still didn't even come close to reaching all the street children. During our prayer time, we had to admit we had to draw the line somewhere. There were boundaries, financial and physical. We couldn't care for all the children in the city every day of the week. Since we had been such adamant visionaries, this fact was hard to accept, but we had no choice.

Our vision didn't change, nor did our goal that not one child would have to live on the street and that all of them would receive support. But we now saw this as a long-term goal, and for the present we had to strategize so that we would be able to keep going. We decided to close Rescue House two days a week. The entire staff would devote all of Friday morning to prayer and fasting and seeking God's guidance for the work with the children. This would give us an opportunity to pray specifically for those children who, because of our ministry, were now off the street. Friday afternoon would be free time, and during the evening we would all hit the streets for evangelism. We would also be closed on Saturday so that we could all have a day off.

Sunday would remain a regular workday because we had opportunities to work together with local churches and speak to Sunday school classes. Sunday was also a good day to visit the families of street children. If the children's parents held jobs, they were usually off on Sunday. The children who came to Rescue House on Sunday could take a shower and then come along with us to church. Our schedule was still full, but it proved to be a vast improvement. With renewed strength and energy we continued to strive to help as many children as possible.

During the first few months that Rescue House was open, hundreds of children came through our doors. We would later report that within the first year we reunited over one hundred children with their families, and after two years, most of them were still at home. However, at the present time we saw children who had no relatives at all or whose problems at home were such that they couldn't return. Once we received the permit to house children, we did take a number of these boys in.

With the staff increase, the house was filled to the brim. Marcos, Jabu, and Elen-Cleber slept on a mattress on the floor in the living room. The boys picked up their bed early in the morning before the waiting multitude outside burst in. Marcos made remarkable progress, and within a few months moved to the base to take the DTS course. His space at Rescue House was immediately taken by another boy.

The time had come to look for larger quarters with more space for additional boys who could stay until they were able to live independently. We were convinced that this was a God-inspired plan. Eagerly we scanned newspapers and visited real estate agents and private owners who had property for sale. The only deterrent, and one that kept us awake at times, was our having no idea how we were going to finance a larger home. Downtown buildings—especially the kind we had in mind—were very expensive. And we needed a building that was large enough to house twenty-five children and twenty staff members. Little did we know, however, that God had even bigger plans.

Financially, God had always come through for us. There were times when we had very little cash; other times we *did* have sufficient funds, but God had asked us to give them away. Now, however, we needed a much larger amount than we had ever previously needed. Whenever I thought about it, I broke out in a cold sweat. It was no longer our own family we were concerned about. We had twenty coworkers who would also be affected by our decision. The responsibility weighed heavily on our hearts.

TWENTY

Opposition

"JOHAN, look here. This sounds interesting."

With a furrowed brow Johan looked at the newspaper's real estate ad I just pointed out to him. For weeks we had searched and looked at dozens of homes. We hadn't seen anything suitable. It was evening, our children were asleep, and Johan had just made a pot of tea. He read the ad out loud: "2,300 sq. ft. property in downtown area." He glanced up at me.

"I already called," I confessed. "There's a house on the property and a school with eight large classrooms, but it's in such poor shape the owner is asking for the value of only the property, not the buildings."

"I assume it's not livable then, if the owner admits that much."

"Probably." We had already seen several buildings that we felt were not habitable but the owners had insisted were in excellent shape, so in what kind of condition would this building be?

"Okay, add it to the list we're going to look at tomorrow afternoon. It wouldn't hurt to drive by."

"F I F T Y thousand dollars. It's a bargain," the real estate agent gushed as he opened the door. We were standing in front of a long, narrow building. On the left side ran a narrow corridor covered with corrugated green plastic sheets. To the right were the classrooms. The narrow hallway had been the only available playground. The house in the front section was worn but boasted three small bedrooms. The entire front facade was missing. The doors hung lopsided on their hinges, and the wooden floors displayed several gaping holes. The walls were in fairly good shape and had small, paint-splattered windows. The commodes were missing in most of the bathrooms, and judging by the smell, it was obvious the water had been cut off for a long time.

The real estate man gave us a jubilant look. "Well? What do you think?"

Hesitating, we looked at each other. Actually, it was a great building. All those classrooms would make excellent bedrooms for the street children. The lounges could be remodeled into sleeping quarters for the staff. The old house in front was a palace compared to the tiny servant quarters in back of Rescue House we now occupied.

The sun broke through a cloudy sky.

"Of course you realize the whole building needs to be bulldozed. Then you can build a great new home," the realtor stated matter-of-factly.

He assumed that since we were foreigners we were loaded. The truth was, we didn't have the nerve to tell him that all we had managed to save was fifteen thousand dollars and we didn't have a clue where the rest would be coming from. With Brazil's high inflation, it's customary to pay cash for homes, or maybe in three monthly installments. If we bought it, it would be an enormous step of faith. We would have to move in right away and then slowly try to resurrect the structure.

"Well?" he waited expectantly.

"It looks okay. We'll call you," Johan put him off. We were afraid he would raise the price if we seemed too eager. But my heart was singing: This is it! This is the place we've been looking for! It was even larger and closer to the downtown area than we had anticipated.

We began some serious prayer times with our team and invited Jim and Pamela to take a look at the property before we made a final decision. Everyone loved it! Initially, some of the staff wondered about the wisdom of getting a home in the city. Wouldn't it be better to buy a farm, where the children could play outside and work the soil and learn how to handle animals?

It sounded like a good idea, but when we began to pray about it, we felt that God wanted us to have a home in the city. That way the children wouldn't be completely removed from their familiar territory, could attend local schools, and would have a vast choice of educational opportunities, and it would be easier for them to find their way back into society. After all, they were city children and had to learn how to live in the city.

Another important point was that in the city it would be easier to work with local churches. The children could become members of a church, and we hoped that churches would be motivated to work with street kids and see our ministry as an example. We would be more visible in the city than way out in the country. One night when Johan took a walk to pray about it some more, God gave him the best reason of all.

Lord, is this really what You want us to do? Should we buy this old school in the city?

It was dark, and even though city noises filled the air, Johan heard only the soft voice of the Lord: *Johan, I love these children more than you do. I want to give you this building in the city. Don't worry about the funds.*

God was behind this! What else did we need?

"Twenty-five thousand down and twenty-five thousand over the next three months," Johan offered the real estate man.

The short, stocky man seemed surprised. "The price is fifty thousand. Why don't you pay it all at once?"

"We don't have it yet, but within three months we'll pay it all," Johan announced with great confidence.

"Well," began the realtor, "you folks were the first to see it, but now someone else is interested and can pay it all up front. I'm afraid the owner will prefer to sell it to him if you can't come up with the whole amount."

Oops! I froze. Johan had been calling lots of people and had managed, through sacrificial gifts from friends and family and our own savings, to scrape together twenty-five thousand dollars. Where was the other half to come from? We hoped many would respond to our newsletter I had just mailed. But mail was slow, and we didn't expect any response for a month and a half or so.

"No," Johan replied firmly, "the balance will be paid in three months."

The real estate man shook his head.

"I don't think you can buy it, then." For another ten minutes he tried to persuade us, but when he realized we were not about to change our minds, he sighed and picked up his briefcase. "Give me a call on Monday. If it's still available, you might have a chance."

On Monday we were told, "Call again on Wednesday. The other buyer hasn't made up his mind, but since he's paying cash he has preference."

On Wednesday we heard, "Call back Saturday. If the other buyer still hasn't decided, it's yours."

"J E A N N E T T E, what shall I do?" Johan inquired. "I promised the YWAM leaders at Curitiba months ago that I would be teaching there for a week. The sale of the building is still up in the air, but I do feel I need to go."

Curitiba is over a thousand miles from Belo Horizonte and has, like so many Brazilian cities, big problems with street kids. It's a twenty-hour bus trip. Johan would have to leave on Saturday and not get back until the following Saturday.

"Go ahead and go. I'll keep in touch with the real estate man. Who knows—I may buy that building while you're gone," I joked.

On Saturday, the real estate man informed me, "Call back on Tuesday. The owner has given the other party until Monday evening to make up his mind."

Then on Tuesday he told me, "Come over tomorrow to sign the contract."

"Excuse me?"

"The other buyer decided to let it go. You can sign the contract tomorrow."

Wow! I knew it! Didn't God tell us? The building was ours!

When I told the staff they erupted into wild applause and whistles. We were sitting in the kitchen, and tea towels and plastic plates suddenly flew through the air. Someone picked up a guitar, and within seconds swinging Brazilian worship songs echoed through the house. Brazilians like to celebrate.

I saw Toos's jaw drop. Toos had just arrived from the Netherlands, where she had faithfully attended church. However, Rescue House was full of surprises for her. She had listened intently that morning as several people had prayed and asked God what they should pray for. The team had waited quietly until several people spoke up about what they believed God wanted them to pray for: Pray for Junia, a street girl, for the church in Bogota, Colombia, for the *Anastasis,* and for the owner of the school building.

"Does God talk to you?" an amazed Toos had asked me later. "I've never heard Him."

I had tried to explain that God could speak to us in various ways—through the Bible, circumstances, or sometimes a sudden thought.

"But don't my thoughts come from me? I mean—I'm the one who thinks them," she had replied, her large gray eyes meeting mine.

"Yes, some thoughts are ours, others are whispered by the devil, and still others are from God. If you ask God to help you to be quiet and you forbid the devil and his demonic forces to influence you, God will sometimes speak directly to your heart."

Deep in thought, Toos had twirled her long blonde hair around her fingers. With a deep frown she had said softy, "I don't think I know God that way."

Now she watched in astonishment as our Brazilian staff burst into exuberant singing.

"Say, Toos, didn't God tell us the school building would be ours? You see? He does what He says." Cleides grabbed Toos's arm and spun her around. It was a funny sight—Cleides, a young, short woman dancing with tall, blonde Toos, who began to laugh in spite of herself.

It had been a busy day. Around fifty children had shown up and kept us going the entire day. After the last one finally left, I was setting the table for dinner back in our tiny home when someone knocked on the door. Outside was Toos. She was crying.

"Jeannette, I don't know God," she wept. "I have always lived for myself, but I don't want to do that anymore. I want to know God the way you do and trust Him like you all do."

Pleasantly surprised, I gave her a hug.

"Toos, that's terrific! Come in and let's talk about it."

She sat down at the table, where her tears splashed between the dinner plates as I explained that the Lord Jesus Christ had died for us so that we can be forgiven and have a personal relationship with God. That night, Toos prayed with me and gave her life to the Lord.

"According to the Bible, you are now born again and my sister in the Lord. Shall we go and tell the others?"

Toos was hugged by exuberant staff members, who felt that this called for another celebration. The guitar was strummed, and the fast-paced Brazilian worship songs again filled the house and overflowed into the streets.

That night I had trouble falling asleep. Too bad Johan was so far away; he still didn't know about the house. I was looking forward to giving him all the details when he got home on Saturday. Silently I prayed, *Lord, this has been a great day! Toos is now Your child, and tomorrow we're buying a house. Thank You! Thank You, Lord!*

I felt that nothing could go wrong now. Wasn't God on our side? For a moment I had forgotten that the devil uses setbacks to discourage us. The next morning I was rudely awakened.

"Jeannette, our van is gone!"

Had I forgotten to set the brake last night? Our street was quite steep and ran into a busy shopping area. I quickly threw on some clothes and ran outside. At the curb some of the staff huddled in agitated conversation.

"I'm sure it was stolen. I already went to the bottom of the street. It's not there," Antonio, who often drove the van, said with a worried look.

Stolen? It didn't sink in. That was impossible! We needed that car every day to distribute food on the street. We also used it to pick up our weekly fruit and vegetable supplies donated by some generous grocers. Often the food filled every inch of the van! It would be impossible to do any of these things without that van. Stolen?

Anger rose up inside me. Who would have the nerve to steal our van right from under our noses? And today, of all days! The day we would be signing the contract and spending our very last nickel on this new building. A secondhand VW van would cost at least eight thousand dollars. It probably was already on its way to be sold in Paraguay, or repainted in some garage, or stripped for parts. I was aware of the statistics on recovering stolen cars in Brazil, and they were not encouraging.

What should I do? I wished that Johan were here! Without that van we couldn't do a thing. Was I supposed to cancel the building contract and get another van instead?

"Antonio, would you call the police and report this? Let's all go inside and pray."

I didn't want to give in to my present feeling of defeat. Wasn't God with us? I saw Toos sitting in a corner of the kitchen.

Lord, please show Toos and us that You do care for us. It's easy for You to provide the finances for another van, I prayed silently. Or—and this would be an even greater miracle—God could return our stolen van! Isn't He omnipotent? I felt my faith and trust rise up once again.

"Today is a day for rejoicing," I announced a few minutes later. "We are going to buy a home, where we'll help hundreds of children get off the streets in the coming years. It's a miracle the owner didn't sell it to someone else, even though he really tried. I believe that God kept this building just for us. It's not difficult for God to perform another miracle. He can return our van or provide funds for another vehicle. Let's trust Him."

The staff nodded in agreement. One after the other they prayed out loud and expressed their faith in God.

"And, Lord, please forgive those thieves, and thank You for taking care of us," I heard Toos pray.

That afternoon I went with Jim to see the owner of the property and signed the contract. God had rewarded our step of faith. Soon funds for the second payment of twenty-five thousand dollars began to arrive. They came from churches, schools, family, friends, and people we didn't even know. The Dutch Christian TV station also contributed generously. Every penny we needed arrived on time.

The icing on the cake came two weeks later when the police called. "We've found your van. It's in good shape. You can pick it up this afternoon."

TWENTY-ONE

A House with Three Walls

O U R new home was christened *Casa Restauração,* or Restoration House. We prayed that many street children would recover here from spiritual, mental, and physical wounds. As soon as we received the keys, we moved in with two of our staff, Paulo and Eduardo.

The boys settled into a classroom at the back of the building, and our family finally encountered life in a "real" home. The fact that it was extremely dilapidated and an entire wall was missing in the living room didn't bother us. A bricklayer had already come by to offer his services, and little by little we would fix and clean up the whole structure.

Jan and Sofia and their two children, who up until then had been living in our house at the base, moved to the city into our old colorful servant quarters behind Rescue House. They replastered and painted the walls, and with those awful colors from the previous tenant gone, the building was transformed into a charming little dwelling. They took charge of the children in the workshop and created innovative projects, which the children thought were great.

We had been in our new home three weeks when the bricklayer began work on the inside walls. Every morning I covered our beds with large pieces of plastic, which, come evening, were covered with a thick layer of sand and dust. The children loved our new abode. They could play hide-and-seek and other fun games throughout the building. Michele's favorite spot was the large heap of cement mix the bricklayer had dumped in the hallway. It was her private sandbox, where she baked all kinds of cookies and pastries. The fact that they were all filthy dirty every night didn't bother the children at all.

Johan finally managed to get one of the old showers to work. It was also our only faucet. We used it to shower and fill buckets of water for the dishes, which I, in the absence of a counter or table, washed while on my knees on the floor. We also needed buckets of water to flush the toilet. Living in such primitive quarters demanded lots of energy, and every night I was wiped out.

Johan had been invited by a YWAM base in Bogota, Colombia, to teach about our work with street children. Bogota has its share of homeless children, and a small team had just opened a home for them. I didn't look forward to having Johan gone for more than a week. The ministry at Rescue House would continue under the leadership of Cleides, who was very reliable and knew how to handle the children. She capably intervened in fights and quarrels and even got the biggest ones to help with the dishes. It was amazing how those children, like little lambs, did everything Cleides told them to do. Her greatest gift, however, was her ability to tell Bible stories. Spellbound, the children hung on her every word. No, I didn't have to worry about the ministry at Rescue House.

The problem was our new home. The bricklayer was much slower than we had expected, and even though we were now able to close our bedroom doors, the outside wall of the living room was still missing. It was easy for anyone to scale the fence surrounding our property and break in. Several street gangs knew about our new home. What if they decided to pay me a visit in the middle of the night while Johan was in Colombia?

Johan wasn't worried. "No way! It's very safe here, and if you see someone climb over the fence, just call Eduardo or Paulo."

"But they are way in the back," I protested.

"You're in the safest possible place—the place God wants you to be," Johan reminded me.

Well, that was true. I knew that God could shield the children and me from danger, even though we lived in the center of a city with four million citizens and even though our house had only three walls. Nevertheless, I was glad when Toos offered to move in with me for the week. The children were crazy about her and loved her no-nonsense approach. We all tried to make our home as livable as possible. Things were actually taking shape, and I began to feel quite at home. Toos and I had become close friends, and she was a tremendous help during this time. We had many long talks about faith and God. Her eagerness to learn was a joy to both of us.

When Johan returned, we decided to take in a street kid named Vitor. Paulo offered to disciple Vitor, but he hadn't been a Christian very long himself. He was raised in a poor family in one of the slums. His dad came home drunk every night, and it didn't take Paulo long to figure out that he had better make himself scarce. He was an excellent soccer player and immersed himself in the sport. Soon he became one of the most popular teenagers in the neighborhood. Even though he was shy, he had plenty of girlfriends.

When he was barely sixteen, he had gotten one of the girls pregnant. Paulo didn't love the girl, but when his daughter was born, his mother offered to care for the baby. Paulo wasn't about to marry the girl or live with her, but a year later she bore him another child, a boy this time. Paulo was only seventeen, and his mother objected to one more child. She arranged with the girl to take turns caring for the babies.

Paulo and his mother fought constantly. Paulo had come to the end of his rope. His life wasn't going the way he had envisioned it at all. He had made a mess of it, an even bigger mess than his father had made of his own life. He determined to focus on his soccer career and in a few years was asked to join a well-known soccer team. Even though soccer had become his life, deep down he knew that something was missing.

Then Paulo had met some Christians, and soon he knew that he had found the God he had been seeking—the God who had created him and wanted to be his Father, the kind of God Paulo wanted to follow. Paulo had been tremendously relieved when he heard that the Lord Jesus Christ had died for his sins, and he had decided to start all over again, this time with God at the helm. He had taken the DTS course at the base and had now been with us for six months. He had done well, and Johan decided to give him a chance. Paulo could disciple Vitor while Johan was discipling Paulo. Paulo and Vitor became best friends.

Soon we took in additional children. Jorge, the hyperactive teenager at Rescue House who felt that God wanted him to be a missionary to the Amazon Indians, was one of them. Regrettably, he didn't last long. On the street *he* decided when and what to eat, when to go to sleep, and what to do every day. Now he was expected to get up early in the morning like everyone else.

"Why, for heaven's sake? For a Bible study?" Grouchy, Jorge would turn over in bed. "You go ahead. I'll join you when I feel like it."

After two weeks he decided to leave and go back to the streets, where he didn't have to take orders from anyone.

We wondered what we should do. We didn't hold these children prisoners, and if they weren't motivated to stay, nothing could keep them. Paulo and Vitor had spent much time with Jorge and were frustrated.

"What have I done wrong?" Paulo asked with tears in his eyes.

Feeling helpless, we shook our heads. "I don't know, Paulo," Johan said. "I don't know if it's us or the way we approach these children, but we're doing our best." He gave Paulo a compassionate look. "Let's pray that God will protect Jorge. I believe that God can bring him back. Isn't it strange how he was always telling us that God called him to work with the Amazon Indians while we had never even talked about that?"

"Yes, I thought that was very interesting. Where did he get that idea?"

"If this is really from God, he'll be back." Johan put his hand on Paulo's sagging shoulders. Paulo blamed himself for Jorge's departure, but we believed that he had done what he could. I prayed that God would speak to him and encourage him.

The team at Rescue House continued to work hard, and every week more children were reunited with their families or admitted to

Restoration House. Eight boys were living with us, and Paulo had acquired two additional helpers. If this trend continued, the school would soon be too small to be our home!

"JOHAN, I read a notice that building safety codes are going to be tightened next year. If you submit the remodeling plans before December 31, they may still be approved." Eduardo had just returned from another of the many visits he had made to the city hall to pick up all the papers needed for the purchase of the property. His announcement resulted in an animated conversation.

"You have got to take advantage of this. This is a golden opportunity. Perhaps we should add one or two stories."

An architect examined the walls and pillars and determined that everything was sturdy and solid enough to safely build two additional floors. For hours I figured and measured the various possibilities of additional rooms and bathrooms. The coolest thing was an apartment for just our family on the first floor. Our present rooms could then be remodeled as a garage or office space. I loved this kind of planning and discussed all my notions with an architect who completed our blueprints before December 31.

Eduardo was asked to oversee the remodeling and make sure that the right building materials were delivered on time so that the work could continue uninterrupted. We hadn't considered the possibility that the whole project could take years. That was just as well, since the irritating sound of the cement mixer right in front of our door was already getting on our nerves.

"JEANNETTE, can you talk to Jose?" Paulo stood at the door that finally graced our living room (the room finally also had an outside wall). I hesitated, but he pleaded, "I don't know what else to do with him."

Jose Wilton had been with us for two weeks. He was a quiet sixteen-year-old. His narrow face was marred by the worst case of acne I had ever seen. Jose had been on the streets since he was seven and didn't know a thing about a "normal" life. In those two weeks he had turned over all our trash cans to search for anything edible. Even though at mealtimes he could eat as much as he wanted, this habit was so ingrained in him that he was unable to break it, even after several reminders from Paulo. But that wasn't the worst of it. In the back of the hallway we kept a large, four-door industrial refrigerator decorated with mirrors. This fridge was like a powerful magnet to Jose who, for his entire life, had had to steal to get food. Night after night, when everyone else was asleep, he could not resist raiding that refrigerator. He often threw up after eating more than his stomach could hold.

That wasn't all. Paulo had three staff girls on his team, and the previous night Jose had been caught peeping in their window.

"Jose, what are you doing, man?"

Alarmed, Jose looked at Paulo.

"Eh…nothing, man!" he stammered, but then his curiosity got the upper hand. "Paulo, don't these broads ever get customers?"

"Customers?"

"Yeah, you know? At night?"

It suddenly dawned on Paulo that the only girls Jose had ever known were prostitutes, and hence Jose thought that all girls lived that way. Jose's jaw dropped when Paulo explained that these girls were not prostitutes and that God had vastly different rules for our lives. Jose could not accept that.

That morning Jose hadn't wanted to get up, and he hadn't wanted any breakfast. He was still full after his midnight visit to the refrigerator and had announced that Paulo could get lost with his programs, Bible studies, math, and soccer.

Paulo gave me a desperate look. "I've tried everything, but nothing sinks in," he lamented.

"Okay. Send him over." I sounded more self-assured than I felt. Jose had been a challenge from the beginning. Challenges fascinated me, but what could *I* do when Paulo, with his incredible patience and gift to put people at ease, had gotten nowhere with Jose? Paulo had proven to be a great coworker these past few months. With his soft-spoken and friendly manner, he had won the boys' trust and respect. Paulo and Vitor were making great progress.

Relieved, Paulo smiled and said, "Good luck!"

A moment later I heard a soft knock on the door. I said a quick, silent prayer: *Lord, please give me the right words.*

"Hi, Jose, come in. Please sit down."

Jose gave me a hostile look, sat down at the kitchen table, and stared at the floor. A deafening silence followed. Jose squirmed uncomfortably in his chair. In one hand he clutched an open pair of scissors. I started to laugh. Jose eyed me suspiciously.

"I see you have come armed."

Embarrassed, he tried to hide his hand under the table, then studied my face.

"Tell me, why did you come here to live?" I calmly asked him.

After a short silence, still looking at the floor, he whispered hoarsely, "I've lived here for two weeks, and I still don't know what you want from me. I get food, a bed, sheets and a blanket, clothes, and, for the first time in my life, a toothbrush. But what do you want from me in return?"

It suddenly hit me! Life on the streets had molded Jose into a person who didn't know what real love was. The "love" he had known on the street was that of homosexuals who had offered him a meal for sex, or the "love" of the slumlords who, in exchange for a few gold necklaces, offered him some glue so that he could get high. Street love was a lie, but that's all Jose knew.

"Jose, we want you to grow up to be a respected, honest man." As clearly and simply as I could, I explained what the gospel is all about. "The Bible says that God's love is free. We don't have to pay anything for Jesus' love. He loves you just the way you are."

Jose's suspicions were melting.

"Did God *give* you this house for us children?" he asked amazed. "Are you saying we really don't have to pay *anything*? It's all *free*?"

"That's right. God wants to show you how much He loves you, and He wants to take care of you. He feels awful that you had to live on the street."

Pensively, Jose digested this information. Suddenly he smiled. "Okay. Thank you." He put the scissors on the table. "Do you want these?"

Grateful for his responsiveness, I accepted the scissors and figured it wasn't the right moment to ask where they had come from.

"Jose, I do expect you to stick to Paulo's schedule for you guys."

"I'll try, *Tia*," came his solemn reply.

"Shall we pray together?" I prayed that God would help Jose to get to know Him.

Afterward, Jose's face was aglow.

"Thank you, Tia!" He jumped up and ran to a classroom where some of the boys where doing some carpentry. Surprised, I watched him run off. Had he really understood? Then I heard him.

"Hey, you guys! You know what? We don't have to pay anything! They're doing all this because God loves us. Jeannette told me herself!" Jose yelled. Then he ran from room to room, repeating the message.

I was deeply touched.

THINGS weren't going well at school with Dilma.

"Did you know that yesterday during schooltime your daughter was wandering around near the bakery two blocks from here?"

I looked with surprise at the mother of one of Dilma's classmates.

"Really! I took her back myself," the mother said.

This was not the first time we had had problems. I had lost track of the times Dilma had been seen on the playground during school hours. The teacher would send Dilma outside the classroom complaining that Dilma gave her a headache. It was a poor excuse, and it didn't do much for Dilma's schoolwork. The teacher, who made minimum wage, wasn't really interested in the children. For the past six months Dilma hadn't learned a thing. We were very concerned. When I unexpectedly visited her school, I noticed one child, arms folded, staring sadly ahead. The other children were busy writing.

"What's the matter with him?" I asked the teacher.

"Oh, he didn't bring his notebook, so he has to sit with his arms folded the whole afternoon." Her tone was indifferent.

I fumed. I knew the boy's mother. She was very poor but took the trouble to take him to school every day on an hour-and-a-half bus ride each way. While he was in class, she would sit on the steps crocheting things she later sold to get some extra cash. I respected her and was irritated that the school didn't offer her a place inside. What if she knew that all her efforts to get her child an education were being carelessly wasted?

"I don't want Dilma to go back to that school!" I announced at home that night. Some of that raw anger from the afternoon was still alive. Deeply concerned, Johan listened. He agreed with me, but what was our alternative? In the entire city this was the only school for the deaf where they taught sign language. Pamela had suggested several times that we try to find a private tutor for Dilma or start our own school, but I dreaded the latter suggestion. I had no teacher training or experience; I was a nurse. I knew nothing about how to put a curriculum together or what subjects to teach.

Everything was so much simpler for Pieter and Johanneke, who attended a private Christian Brazilian elementary school with high academic standards. The school had over seven thousand students, including seventeen first-grade classes.

I had noticed how well this school was run and decided to speak with the supervisor, a friendly, energetic middle-aged woman. She fully understood my frustration and gave me some names of newly graduated teachers. Great idea! After some calls we found a sweet, private teacher for Dilma. We put a desk in Dilma's room, and our daughter's new school was up and running. We never regretted that decision. Dilma, who had a low IQ and a problem concentrating, made tremendous progress under the woman's personal tutelage. This was also the beginning of a small school for children with disabilities.

"J O S E hasn't come home," a concerned team leader reported to Paulo.

Jose wouldn't be coming home for quite some time. Eventually, we found out what had happened. Jose had often been taunted because of his severe acne. One day, someone said it was probably because he had AIDS. Even though there was no truth to this, it had become his dreaded, secret fear. AIDS was a relatively new disease, and many weird and terrifying stories were circulating on the streets.

A routine procedure for all new residents at Restoration House was a series of simple medical tests for such things as anemia, worms, sexually transmitted diseases, and tuberculosis. A doctor friend assisted us with these procedures and became so involved that she eventually opened a free clinic for street children. Jose had been scared to death of these tests. He was now convinced he had AIDS but didn't dare discuss it with anyone. When his turn at the clinic came and the receptionist started to fill out a standard form on him, he took it as a sign that his suspicions were true. Sobbing, he fled back to the streets. Even though all his tests had come back negative, it would be several months before we would see him again.

In the meantime, the cement mixer droned on for three long years, but when two additional floors had been added and all remodeling was finally done, I was ecstatic! The building had been transformed. We had a wonderful home with many large windows. It had enough room to house a hundred people. On the ground floor were large sleeping areas for the boys and a few rooms for the staff. The first floor had apartments for us and for additional workers and a meeting hall; the second floor boasted a roof garden, a covered soccer field, and additional dorms for thirty short-term volunteers. The ministry was growing, and so was the staff. The pioneer phase was over.

TWENTY-TWO

Deeper and Wider

"IN RIO de Janeiro 1,451 street children were mur-
dered this year. Recife (a city in northern Brazil) came in a tragic second with 891 murders." The TV anchorman's trained expression was
grave, then quickly changed as he launched into the results of the latest auto races and soccer games. I was shocked that the news of the
death of over two thousand children took less than thirty seconds
while the sports report lasted more than ten minutes.

"If this represents a sample of people's interest, we have a long way
to go," Johan observed dryly.

It was 8:30. Our children were asleep, and with the television now
turned off, silence pervaded our living room.

"Wouldn't it be great if we could send workers to Recife and Rio
and all the other cities that have street children?" I dreamed aloud.

Between the two homes we had twenty coworkers, but with the
enormity of the street problems, we could use multitudes more.

"You know," I began, "I think we could recruit a lot more staff if we offered them some training on street children ministries."

"I'm listening," Johan replied. I knew I had his attention.

"Have you noticed how many people say that they would like to come and help out but never do?" I continued. "I believe a lot of them would come if we could train them."

"Mmm, a very practical type of training," Johan mused. "They could live here in Restoration House. I could teach in the morning, and in the afternoon and evening we could go out on the streets." He got up to get paper and pen.

"Okay. Let's write down what subjects should be included." He bent over his notebook. "A biblical explanation of why it is important to work with children and not just adults."

"Some basic first aid," I added, recalling the dirty and often infected wounds of the children.

"How to be creative. We can teach them how to work with puppets and create stories and skits." Johan's pen raced across the paper.

"We could invite other people to teach about children with mental traumas and..." A vital thought suddenly hit me. "And a doctor to explain about AIDS and other sexually transmitted diseases. I could also teach on abortion." (Officially abortions can't be performed in Brazil, but I had read that an estimated 1.4 million abortions are performed a year anyway.)

I paused, recalling our sit-ins at the Los Angeles abortion clinics. *Oh*, I thought, *if only Christians would understand that every little life that is taken from the womb is actually a person for whom God has made good plans—a person who will never live out the dreams God dreamed. If only Christians would understand their responsibility to reach out to pregnant mothers who are desperate for help and fearful of the future. If Christians would learn to stand next to those mothers and love them and their children, not only in words but especially in practical deeds—perhaps then we could prevent a lot of abortions!*

"After graduation, these students could teach in Sunday schools and in the slums," I dreamed on. "They could share what they have learned with others."

"Excellent! I could also teach planning and management so that workers could go to other cities to start similar ministries."

The list was impressive, and we felt we could easily fill three months to cover the subjects we felt were vital. Eventually, we found out that our course could be taught as an extension course of YWAM's University of the Nations in Hawaii. When the training was officially announced just a few months later, it didn't take long before we had our first twelve students assembled in a large room of Restoration House.

"Welcome to our Rescue and Restore Training School!" Johan was once again facing a group of students. Teaching was definitely one of his gifts, and with his clear explanations and lively gestures he kept his students spellbound for hours.

This was the beginning of a steady stream of hundreds of students who came—and are still coming—to take this course before moving on to full-time work with street children. Some of the students moved to other cities after graduation to work among street children. Most of them stayed with us, however, which made our ministry expand even faster so that we were able to help many additional children.

IN THOSE days 10 to 20 percent of all street children were girls. Up until now we had taken in only boys, but the tragic situation with street girls was an even bigger concern. Even though we had established a home for boys, we now realized that a separate home for girls was a dire necessity. We had never again heard from Sonia. Had she gone into prostitution, or had she moved to another city (which many of the girls did when things got too hot)? We didn't know, but we often prayed for her.

Many other girls also needed help. One of our workers had recently been called to the hospital to see a thirteen-year-old girl, Edna, in ICU. Edna, who was one of our street girls, had been severely burned. We never found out what exactly caused the fight, but one night the gang decided to teach her a lesson. While she struggled, several boys held her down while the others raped her. She was wounded, bleeding, and deeply humiliated. But the worst was yet to come. Suddenly one of the children emptied a bottle of 96 percent alcohol over her. Before she realized what was happening, someone else had lit a match and she had become a living torch. She was still unconscious when some pedestrians took her to the hospital.

"Tia, may I please come and live with you when I get out of here?" Edna asked in a hoarse whisper. Her eyes were pleading. "I don't want to go back to the streets. Please, help me."

Hers wasn't the only cry for help. Almost every day, girls would ask us when we were going to open a home for them. It became a daily prayer request that, it turned out, would be answered quickly.

We found an incredible home! It had functioned as a youth hostel and had sixteen large bedrooms, plenty of bathrooms, and beautiful, cozy living rooms. It was only a five-minute walk from Restoration House, and the owner, a fellow Christian, was willing to sell it to us. Our only problem: where would we get the money? Several weeks later we received a fax from the Netherlands:

> *Are you still thinking of getting a home for girls?*
> *If so, please call. We can donate $120,000!*

That's really what it said! God had laid it on the hearts of people in my country to give specifically toward a home for girls. He had encouraged us once again. We had barely begun to pray for a home for girls, and here we had most of the funds.

A few weeks later, extremely grateful, we opened *Casa Recanto*. *Recanto* means something like "a quiet, cozy place." Here the girls received wonderful, loving care from our dedicated staff. They went through the same training as the boys did at Restoration House. After taking some aptitude tests they attended school, and after graduation, they had several available training options, depending on their talents and interests. Every day began with Bible study and prayer, and soon these broken lives began to heal and bloom.

O N E of the boys who showed up again was Jorge! He appeared at the door one day and asked if he could come back. He had made the decision to leave the street life after all. What's more important, he had also decided to become a Christian! Paulo and all of us were delighted!

Jorge had counted the cost; he gave up his freedom to do whatever he wanted to and decided instead to live his life in obedience to God and allow God to use him. He became a zealous student and was still convinced God wanted him to go to the Amazon Indians. He was still hyperactive, and it wasn't always easy for him to sit still in school and stick to the rules. However, most frustrations were resolved after five in the afternoon on our small, covered soccer field on the roof. After kicking and running after that ball for an hour, pent-up, excess energy dissipated like snow in the sun.

Our staff was no longer limited to people from Brazil or the Netherlands. Newsletters were being mailed to YWAM bases in other countries, and volunteers arrived regularly to stay for one or two months, as Toos had done. Others committed themselves for at least two years. Two of our new people were Daniel and Mati. They had come from the isle of Samoa in the Pacific where we had visited years ago with the *Anastasis*. Daniel was a born leader. His English was better than Mati's, and he usually was the spokesman. He was the livelier of the two, while Mati was the quieter one. Both were amiable and sincere and soon made new friends.

So many things were new and different for Daniel and Mati. Their small island had a population of 178,000, while the city of Belo Horizonte had over four million citizens. Samoa had no street children. If a child became an orphan or other family problems arose, the child would always find a relative to take him or her in. Even though the island was far from wealthy, there was always plenty of rice, fish, and bananas, so no one ever went hungry. Daniel and Mati were well-fed, broad-shouldered, huge guys with bulging biceps. Here, for the first time in their lives, they were seeing hungry people.

One day Daniel and Mati accompanied Johan in the van to distribute to various city locations the daily thirty or so hot dinners wrapped in foil. (We stayed in daily contact with these folks and got to know them well, as we did the new street children. It's much easier to get the new children off the streets before they have become hardened and street-smart.)

Johan parked the car, stopping under an overpass. In a far corner, covered by a torn blanket, were three sleeping young boys. Johan gently shook them awake. This meal would probably be the only one they would get that day, and he didn't want them to miss out. Still sleepy, the boys followed him to the car to get their meal. Suddenly children and adults appeared from all directions.

"Hi, Tio Johan, did you bring anything for me?" Most of the children knew him by name. Soon a crowd had gathered. Mati and Daniel had never seen so much poverty and misery. It was such a shock that they both burst into tears. Johan looked with surprise at the strange sight of these two huge, sobbing men.

"Hey there, Mati and Daniel. Over here. Come and give me a hand." Johan wasn't sure what was going on, but he needed help before the children swarmed into the car to help themselves. He gave each of them a few dinners of rice, beans, and a fried egg. Still crying, the two men began to hand out the food. With each dinner they gave away, their sobs became louder until their huge shoulders were shaking. The surprised children didn't know what to think and timidly accepted their food.

"What's going on, you guys? Something wrong?" Concerned, Johan pulled them aside.

"No, it's okay," Daniel sniffled. "This is so awful. We've never seen anything like it before."

Daniel picked up the last remaining dinners. The only people left in line were some homeless men who were gaping in utter amazement at the two Samoans. Suddenly, they began to cry too. They didn't understand what was going on, but they sensed the Samoans' sadness.

Quickly Johan spoke up. "These men from Samoa have never seen as many problems as you have, and they are shocked and sad, just like God. God never intended for your lives to be like this. He has a different plan for you."

The crowd became quiet. Mati and Daniel got back into the car, but Johan continued. "God wants to give you a new life. You can start all over with Him. He loves you and wants to take care of you."

He scanned the crowd. Never had the children been so quiet. He saw Mati and Daniel in the car, eyes closed, tears still running down their faces. He knew they were praying.

Johan explained to his audience that all the wrong things we've done in our lives have separated us from God like a brick wall, but the Lord Jesus, God's Son, died for us and broke down that wall.

"God is our Father. He created us, and He wants you to turn your life over to Him. If that's what you want, step over here and I'll pray with you."

Several children and adults prayed that afternoon with Johan. It was a special day. Mati and Daniel had shown these people, as no one else could have, how much God loves them. They eventually were able to function in the midst of the abject poverty around them without shedding all those tears. We prayed that our hearts would always remain sensitive and we would never get used to this wretchedness.

"I LIKE to work with the homeless," Eduardo announced. "The adults on the streets are a group all by themselves."

Johan nodded and thoughtfully observed, "This city is like a package wrapped in many layers. Every time one layer comes off, there's another one, and another problem surfaces. First the boys on the street, then the girls, now the homeless adults." He sighed deeply. "Tell me, what do you have in mind?"

Eduardo sat on the edge of his chair and described his dream of inviting the homeless to Rescue House, giving them a shower, clean clothes, and a meal, and then telling them about the Lord.

"I would also like to build a small office on the flat roof of the house to have a quiet place where they could talk, get counseling, pray, and have Bible studies. On Sunday when all the street children are in church and Rescue House is empty, I would like to have an open house for every homeless person who wants to come."

It sounded like a good idea. Eduardo invited a few of these men from the streets, and soon between 120 and 150 showed up at the door of Rescue House every Sunday. Actually, Rescue House was just a small townhouse type of building with a modest living room, but every Sunday the showers, washing machine, and stove did double duty.

OUR teams kept growing. Soon we had almost forty staff members; people from different countries and cultures, each with his or her own background and ideas. It wasn't always easy to lead them. We had never had that many staff workers before, and with all those nationalities there were at times misunderstandings. But we all had the same goal: to be used by God to help street children and the homeless and to show them God's love.

Another thing that wasn't always easy to schedule was enough time for our own children. There was always so much to do, and often people demanded Johan's time morning, noon, and night. Our children went to school only in the morning. They were off during the afternoon but had lots of homework. From first grade on, children were given homework, and their mothers were expected to supervise. At times, my patience was severely tested.

Johan loved his work and was completely immersed in it. Sometimes I envied the street children, students, and staff, who seemed to see more of him than I did. Of course, I immediately felt guilty when I had such thoughts. Wasn't this exactly what God had asked us to do? I told myself I should be grateful to have such a hardworking husband, but during those hectic days I often felt lonely.

As a result I shifted into even higher gear and was determined that next to God, Johan and the children were my top priority. I tried to be as good a mother and wife as I possibly could. However, I also relished my time with the street children and our staff, and thus I often took on more than I could handle. I was in charge of the kitchen, did all the shopping, and put together the menus. I was the nurse for all three of the homes and wrote letters and newsletters, brochures, and forms in Dutch, Portuguese, and English. Every day I discussed Dilma's schedule with her teacher, and often during the evening I wrote simple Portuguese Bible stories for her. I also tried to disciple the new staff members and took time to listen to their problems. At night I was exhausted.

It was a good thing we didn't know then that the ministry was about to explode even more rapidly and demand still more from all of us.

TWENTY-THREE

Street Babies

"J O H A N, hurry! They're going to torch Marcia's baby!"

An out-of-breath staff member rushed into the office. Johan was shocked. He knew Fabiana, the nine-month-old baby of Marcia, a fourteen-year-old street girl. Our staff had invited Marcia several times to move into Recanto House, but Marcia didn't want to hear about it. She enjoyed her street "freedom" too much, and she now had a baby to look after. At times Fabiana received good care and looked just like the doll Marcia had always wanted but never had. At other times, however, Marcia completely forgot she was a mother. She would sniff glue to get high or finish a gallon of cheap wine with her street buddies while Fabiana lay forgotten somewhere in a corner. More than once, other street girls helped out.

Now the baby had been kidnapped. A rival gang had waited for the right moment to snatch the infant. As a rule they wouldn't harm a defenseless baby, but after getting high, these street children could become unimaginably cruel.

Our staff worker had heard that the gang was going to drench Fabiana in paint thinner and light a match. Johan didn't waste a moment but jumped into the car and tore downtown. He saw a group of children in an alley standing in a tight circle around Fabiana, who was lying on the dirty street. The children had forced paint thinner into Fabiana's little mouth and were ready to light a match.

Enraged, Johan grabbed the baby and brought her home. He carefully put her in my arms. We knew she was nine months old, but she looked no more than three months. She was terribly tiny and thin and let out a pitiful wail. I fashioned a little bed for her in one of our bedroom dresser drawers. She fell right asleep. When she woke she numbly stared into space. Nothing made her smile. In fact, when we tried to make eye contact, she would look the other way. Pieter, Johanneke, and Dilma scattered their toys about her, but her only response was that pathetic, thin whine. I had never seen a child this young who had already lost confidence in humanity and who was as frightened as she was.

"She's severely malnourished," the doctor sighed as she bent over the still form of Fabiana. "It's a miracle she's still alive. She needs a lot of love and care."

"JEANNETTE, we would like to adopt Fabiana. We prayed about it and believe this is God's will," one of our coworkers happily announced. She and her husband had a fine family. I was grateful— Fabiana had a future now, after all the pain, neglect, and fear on the street. She was adopted into a loving family. Soon she was making dramatic progress and just a few months later had been transformed into a happy, healthy toddler. Her biological mother, Marcia, didn't do well. She managed to abort her second baby, felt remorseful afterward, and visited her daughter a few times, but eventually she vanished.

"Marcia? She's in jail. She tried to kill one of her friends with a broken bottle," some other children told us.

We saw an alarming increase in the number of pregnant street girls. One day a staff worker counted sixteen very pregnant teens—just in the downtown area. It wasn't because of ignorance or a lack of information; the girls purposely became pregnant. They wanted to have their own little baby to cuddle. However, they were still children themselves and didn't have the slightest sense of responsibility.

Most of the babies died within six months of their birth. We were able to save some of them, like Scarlet, a pathetic, skinny creature her fourteen-year-old mother, Jacqueline, had thrust into our arms after the father, also a street kid, threatened to kill both Jacqueline and the baby. We found a temporary hiding place for Scarlet, and eventually she, too, was adopted.

Many street babies were seriously ill when they arrived at our home and spent a few nights, sometimes months, next to our bed. Johan and I rotated the feedings. Bottles, burps, diaper changes—nothing fazed Johan. Eventually we both became chronically tired. Our daytime activities didn't let up either. Actually, the opposite was true. Our own four children demanded a lot of time. However, in the near future we would be even more pressed for time.

One of our workers one day brought Davi, a four-year-old tyke with deep, infected wounds covering both knees and both hips. It didn't bother Davi; he was paralyzed and didn't feel anything below his waist. He had a huge smile and clutched a large ball in both hands.

"Let's play," he invited me. He let go of the ball and briskly scooted after it. Our children came closer to look him over. When Pieter timidly pushed the ball in Davi's direction, Davi squealed with delight. Our children had to get used to seeing Davi drag along his numb legs, but before long the five children were frolicking on the floor. Davi was having the time of his life.

"Davi is the son of Teresa, a prostitute," the staff member told me. "She asked if he could stay in Restoration House for the weekend. Her boyfriend kicked her out after they had a fight, and she's going to look for a job and another apartment. I said it would be okay."

Teresa never came to pick up her son. At the address she had given, no one had ever heard of her. Then we knew—she had abandoned Davi. When we asked around at some bars, several prostitutes remembered Teresa. Some of them even recalled Davi's birth.

"It was Christmas Day," one of them said. "Davi was born at the brothel with a water head and an open spinal chord. He looked awful.

All crooked. That must have been her punishment. She had given herself abortions eight times."

Little by little the story unfolded. The women had swaddled Davi in some old rags and taken him to the hospital. He needed major surgery, which his mother could not afford.

"I'll tell you what," the surgeon on call had announced after examining Davi at length. "It's Christmas today, no? I have a present for this little guy. I won't charge for the surgery."

Davi had been born on exactly the right day and did well after a six-hour operation. A shunt drained the excess fluid from his head, and the exposed spinal cord was closed. The surgery left an ugly, large scar across his back. However, the nerves below the scar were dead, and Davi would be permanently paralyzed. For the next four years Davi had spent most days in bed in the slum house his mother and her boyfriend occupied. Neighbors said that he had been left alone for days. Several times they called the police. Davi's diet had been nothing but rice, beans, and macaroni. He didn't know what candy was, nor did he want any fruit, vegetables, Popsicles, or even ice cream. He had never tasted it. He didn't like milk either. All he wanted was tea with *pinga*, a sweet, strong alcoholic beverage!

"Shall we adopt him?" Johan asked.

I hesitated. It was fairly easy to find foster care for newborns, but to find a home for a severely disabled four-year-old would be almost impossible. No one dared take the risk. Besides, no health insurance would accept him, and no one knew what future medical costs would be involved.

Was this really from God? I didn't feel ready to make a decision. The struggles I had had in accepting Dilma's limitations were still fresh in my mind. Would we really want to adopt another disabled child and go through similar battles? Was I willing to trust God with yet another child who could be healed only by a miracle? What if there were no miracle for Davi?

It wasn't any easier for me when the neurologist predicted that Davi might not survive his childhood or teen years. Was I willing to adopt a child we might have to bury in a few years? Could we as a family survive something like that? The whole matter kept me awake many a night. God didn't seem to give us a clear answer, and I continued to hesitate and waver.

We heard about a family in the States who had adopted three children with similar disabilities as Davi's and were looking to adopt a fourth. They felt that this was their calling and even had bought a home next to a hospital that specialized in such cases.

"Shall we try this family first? Maybe Davi was meant for them and God is using us as a middleman, as He has done with so many other babies."

Johan agreed, but our children strongly objected. They had come to love this lively, cheerful little guy and felt we should adopt him ourselves.

"It will be a couple of months before his papers are ready," I consoled them. "We can still enjoy him for a while."

Davi adapted incredibly fast. Not once did he ask for his mother, and he relished the attention he got from our family and coworkers. Johan mounted a little seat in front of his bike and took him along for rides. Davi's screams of delight could be heard for blocks.

The U.S. couple agreed to the adoption, and many letters went back and forth across the ocean. Months passed as bureaucratic red tape slowed progress to a snail's pace. Davi shared a room with Pieter. Above his bed I had pinned some pictures of his new parents. At night he prayed for them. He seemed to understood they were going to adopt him.

After many months of paperwork it came as a complete surprise when the prospective parents suddenly changed their minds. One of their children had been severely ill, and for months his little life had hung in the balance. Emotionally, it was such a trauma they didn't think they could handle another child.

Now what? Start all over to find potential adoptive parents? By this time Davi had been with us for over a year, and we had all grown very attached to this little guy with his open, friendly personality. Was he meant for us after all?

Lord, I wish You would speak more clearly, I sighed.

I was afraid, I was worried, and I was lonely. Johan was gone for three weeks, speaking in several cities in northeastern Brazil about our work with street children.

"Jeannette, I wouldn't mind adopting him," he had said on the phone. "Pray about it."

We had already discussed it so often. Johan didn't see as many potential difficulties as I did, but we had agreed that we needed to hear from God so that we could be sure we could handle it. I preferred a written note from God and hadn't been in this much turmoil for a long time.

Jeannette, you're asking the wrong question. I am not forcing you.

I suddenly heard that still, small voice in my heart.

"Excuse me, Lord? What if we *don't* adopt him? Won't You be terribly disappointed with me?"

Jeannette, I love you. I won't leave you. I understand if you're afraid. It's not a sin if you don't adopt him! It's not a commandment.

A heavy load was lifted from my already burdened soul.

I want you to know I'll always be with you, no matter what you choose.

An astounding revelation hit me: God didn't promise a healing, He didn't even promise that Davi would survive the next few years, but He *did* promise to be with us and not leave us.

I would not cease to be a child of God if we did not adopt Davi. God wouldn't force me, but He promised to always be with me. He would be there through difficult times; He would be there if Davi became ill or died. It was so simple! Hadn't Jesus made that same promise just before His ascension to heaven? Suddenly, that awesome promise came to life: *God with us!* He's there for our future cares and our future sorrows. My "head knowledge" had suddenly become "heart knowledge." When Johan called the next day I told him that Davi was ours.

Many other street babies and toddlers passed through our bedroom. Eventually, we found adoptive homes for all of them. Take Dayane, a baby who had fallen into a fast-flowing open sewer just when some of our workers passed by. In the nick of time she escaped certain drowning. During the first three weeks with us, she was admitted to the hospital three times with double pneumonia. Doctors didn't give her much hope, but she made it and is now part of a wonderful family. Her parents are also YWAM missionaries.

Or take Matheus, who was born with a harelip and cleft palate. We kept him at our home for almost a year but then found loving parents for him.

So many street babies were coming to our doorstep that we eventually made it a separate branch of our ministry by setting aside a few rooms and arranging for staff to rotate round-the-clock shifts. This gave us a chance to take care of the growing bags under our eyes.

TWENTY-FOUR

A Great Injustice

W I T H mixed feelings I said good-bye to Johan when he departed on yet another trip. This time he was going all the way to Budapest for a conference hosted by the YWAM university.

I was happy for him, but it also meant double duty for me, especially managing our own family. I was grateful that Carla had offered to stay with me. Our children loved her. During the short time she had been here, she had become a dear friend and a popular "auntie" to the children. She would be primarily responsible for Davi's care. Even though he was small for his age, he was pretty heavy, and when I lifted him into the tub it felt like he weighed a hundred pounds. My back was beginning to protest loudly.

It was a quiet Friday evening. The children had been asleep for hours. Suddenly our peace was shattered. It was the infamous night the local police had brutally attacked and arrested our gentle Mati. After a wild chase we had found him bruised, bleeding, and collapsed in a corner of the darkened police precinct on a cold, hard floor. A livid cop had pushed me into a small room and slammed the door shut after turning up the volume of a small TV set. Nervously, I paced back and forth in the stuffy space, hardly able to realize what was happening. It was like a very bad dream.

Jeannette, you're crazy! I heard a soft whisper. *Do you realize what danger you're in?*

Angry, I tried to ignore that voice. I recognized it. It was the voice of the one forever waiting in the wings, ever ready to discourage me.

You can't help street kids. It's a hopeless cause. You're better off in Holland.

I knew I shouldn't give in to his taunts. Confused, I turned my back to the blaring television and walked over to the small, barred window.

"Lord God, I need you!" I whispered into the dark night.

Suddenly, I heard the voices of our coworkers who had stayed in the car. They were yelling under my window.

"Jeannette! Hurry! They're taking Mati again!" There was panic in their voices.

"And, Lord, please help Mati," I quickly prayed.

Angry and determined, I threw my full weight against the door. It hadn't been locked at all, and it flew open. Under the loud protests of the cursing police officer, I ran outside to once again see that gray police car take off. However, at that very moment our military police friend's car turned into the street and stopped right in front of us.

"Hurry, they're gone again!" we yelled. I jumped into the passenger seat of his car, and this time two cars followed in pursuit—the second wild chase that night. The patrol car with Mati tore through the center of the huge city. I wished we could go faster. The officers in Mati's car could still kill him. My white-knuckled hands were cold and clammy. Finally, the car screeched to a halt in front of another dark, dingy police station. I had no idea in which part of the city we were. When we burst through the door, we found Mati slumped in a chair. He looked deathly pale.

I rushed over to him. Determined that nobody was going to stop me this time, I quickly threw an arm around his shoulders.

"Mati, how are you?"

His large brown eyes filled with tears.

"I'm in a lot of pain," he whispered.

"Mati, I'm going to do everything I can to get you home as soon as possible," I promised.

He nodded with a look of gratitude.

I marched to the lone officer seated behind a large desk in the semidark room. Silently he looked me over. The other police officers had all mysteriously disappeared. This man was trying to intimidate me, but I didn't give him the pleasure. Besides, I was so livid I was fearless. They had beaten up *my* Mati!

At first, the officer was going to lock up Mati, but through the intervention of our friend the lieutenant colonel, he finally decided to let him go. With a scowl he got up from behind his desk as though he couldn't wait for us to leave.

"Excuse *me!* You want us to leave just like that?" I faced the man head-on. "They beat up Mati, and now we can just leave? No way! Those police officers are going to pay for this! I want to file a complaint!"

A lawyer arrived—an old, nervous man with a tired, pale face. One of our staff had called him for advice. When he heard we were planning to file a complaint against the police department, he turned right around in his tracks. No way! Too risky.

"Wait! What do you mean—too dangerous?" I tried to grab his sleeve. With a quick motion he ran his forefinger across his throat, turned around, and vanished into the night. Incredulous, I watched the door close behind him. This wasn't possible. A great injustice had been done, and nobody would be held accountable?

Our lieutenant colonel friend hesitated. In a few months he would retire, and this whole matter was outside his jurisdiction. Yet he made the courageous decision to file an official complaint. The desk officer almost fell off his chair. Law officers in Brazil always protect each other.

Over the loud protests of the cursing officer, two of us helped Mati up and gently guided him out of the shabby office. I was so outraged my legs were shaking. Our next stop was a military hospital to get documentation of Mati's injuries. (In Brazil all police incidents are handled by the military police.) Poor Mati was covered with nasty bruises and ugly welts and could hardly walk. We carefully eased him into the car.

At the hospital a doctor examined him thoroughly and advised that he be admitted. Briefly we considered that option. We didn't trust these people; even our lieutenant colonel friend didn't trust them. There were too many police officers involved.

"No thanks. We'll take him home."

The doctor shrugged and handed me his report. Eagerly I took it.

Finally, we were free to go. Back outside, we deeply inhaled the cool morning air. Mati was free! It was 7:30 in the morning.

We called some of the news media about Mati's treatment by the police. Within the hour newspaper reporters and radio and television crews had swarmed Restoration House. They all wanted exclusive interviews. I talked to them for hours. Mati, unable to sleep, decided to get out of bed and give them some interviews too. Carefully, he pulled up his T-shirt. Cameras zoomed in on the welts and bruises covering his abdomen and his back.

"Mati, why did they do this to you? Didn't they know you were a foreigner and a missionary?"

"Oh sure, they knew." Soft-spoken Mati with his heavy accent carefully related how they had confiscated his papers on the way to their first stop, the bus station, and joked about killing a Samoan.

I hadn't heard *that*! What in the world had gotten into these men! The cluster of microphones was pushed even closer to Mati's face so that not one word would be lost.

"I was blindfolded with my own T-shirt; then they pointed five guns at me. Two to my temples, two to my chest, and one in back of my throat." His voice faltered. "I really thought this was it..." He swallowed hard.

"So what are you going to do? Are you going to take revenge?"

With a faint smile he said, "No, not revenge. I'm a Christian. The issue is not revenge; the issue is justice."

Cameras flashed; pens flew across paper. I was proud of Mati.

Suddenly I realized how dead tired I was. Feeling dizzy, I stood up.

"Okay, you guys, I'm going to my room," I told our office staff. "Tell those press people I'll be available again in an hour."

Exhausted, I fell into bed. I desperately wished that Johan were here, yet gratitude filled my heart.

Thank You, Lord, for Your protection, I prayed silently.

The next day, a Sunday, to my great surprise, twenty-seven pastors and elders from various churches gathered at our doorstep.

"We're here to encourage you," one began. "The street children are not your problem. They are our problem. We're so sorry about what happened."

Moved, I invited them in. Right from the start of our ministry we had prayed that local churches would see their responsibility and get involved, but up to this point only a few of the three thousand churches in Belo Horizonte had done anything. We had prayed that our example would motivate them into action.

Now here was a group of clergy who had hastily found others to preach for them so that they could come and encourage and pray for us. How touching. They all agreed that we had done the right thing in filing a complaint. They even offered to write a letter of protest and later that week arranged for another interview, which was covered by all five national TV stations in Brazil.

That same Sunday a bus filled with military police parked in front of our door. The MPs spread out across the entire street and stayed on guard for a week. I wasn't too happy about that and decided to call the chief of police.

"Are they here to guard us or intimidate us?" I asked him.

"Madam, I don't know. We didn't order this."

Frustrated, I put the phone down. Even the chief seemed to have no control over his own troops. Everyone did as he pleased.

As a child I was told that whenever I lost my way I should ask a police officer, who was sure to help and could always be trusted. But in this country we didn't know whom to trust or not to trust. Undoubtedly, there were many honest police officers, as our lieutenant colonel friend had often reminded us. Many, however, supplemented their meager salary of seventy-five dollars a month by engaging in criminal activities. It was a known fact that in Rio de Janeiro shopkeepers, who were losing business because of the presence and activities of street children, would pay police officers up to one hundred dollars for every street kid they killed. That was but one way the police supplemented their income during their night shifts.

During this time I had spoken several times with Johan on the phone. He was shocked and wanted to come home right away, but his flight was booked for the following week. It was hard for Johan not to be able to do anything except pray. That he did with all his might. He also described the incident to those at the conference in Budapest, and the people there prayed for us as well. People from all over the world were attending, including several journalists. As a result we didn't just have Brazilian news coverage, but the incident was also reported in the United States, Canada, New Zealand, England, and Holland. Even the Dutch Christian television phoned for an interview. It took place at three in the morning Brazil time, but I didn't mind. I prayed that all the publicity would help resolve the case and curb police brutality against street children and the people who were trying to help them.

Johan gave me the name of another lawyer in Belo Horizonte. That Sunday afternoon Mati and I were to meet him at police headquarters. The new lawyer immediately agreed to join us. I suppressed a smile when I first saw him. He came with a colleague, and they looked like two bodybuilders. What a difference from the nervous, fretting little man we had met before. These two big, muscular young men looked very imposing. When we walked through the hallways under the hateful stares and glances of dozens of military police, I was glad to have these two Tarzans at our side.

Mati still walked with difficulty. Photographers surrounded us. The MPs were disgusted, and the air was loaded with hostility. An angry-looking guard nodded toward a waiting room. I wondered: Were we in danger? Could they do something to us here, right in their own headquarters? Were we caught in the lions' den? I didn't know what to think anymore. Promising an interview, I asked the photographers and journalists to stay until after the case had been decided. Now the MPs were boiling mad.

An officer entered the little waiting room, pulled up a chair very close to us, and sneered. "So you want to make our police officers look like fools, eh?"

"No, not look like fools," I answered calmly, but I was getting steamed again. "We want to see justice done."

Mati sized up his opponent and then with a steady voice related everything that had happened that night. While Mati was speaking, the officer interjected sarcastic and disparaging remarks, but Mati was not intimidated. I was relieved and noticed that Mati's dignified demeanor and self-confidence were beginning to have an effect on the officer. Our entire team back home were on their knees praying. I was grateful. The peace we experienced was the peace of God.

The following Friday night Mati felt well enough to join the street team. TV cameramen were on his tail recording his every step. It gave me a feeling of safety: I didn't believe the police would try anything with all those cameras around. The street kids welcomed Mati as their hero. Now Mati knew firsthand what they had to endure. They looked up to him with pride. He was their best friend.

"Mati, why don't you go back to Samoa?" a surprised journalist asked.

"God called me here to help street kids," Mati answered in his own quiet way, "and now I can really identify with what these kids have to go through." He paused and then declared, "I'm staying!"

A few days later I picked up Johan at the airport. We had both counted the days. I was feeling a little hesitant. Did Johan approve of the way I had handled things? So much had happened, and suddenly our ministry had gone international. Wouldn't he have done a much better job with all those interviews? His command of the Portuguese language was better than mine, and he always expressed himself so well. He was also good at solving problems. Did he feel I acted correctly in this crisis?

I should not have worried. Johan ran toward me and threw his long arms around me in a tight bear hug. I relaxed and felt safe again. His suitcase stood almost forgotten on a cart next to him.

"You are the most terrific wife in the whole world!" he whispered in my ear.

I was at peace—we were alive, we loved each other, and we were serving God together.

T H E court case dragged on. From a long lineup Mati had positively identified ten officers. It was determined without a doubt that all of them had been present at the scene that night, but only four were selected as scapegoats to be legally prosecuted. I wondered why the others were being protected. Exactly one year later, two of those four men were sentenced to two years in prison, another one to nine months. The fourth one, a rather short fellow, was dismissed "because," the judge declared, "he's too little to have done much harm."

Even though the sentences were ridiculously short and the police in question wouldn't lose their jobs and would be back on the streets after their release, a precedent had been set. What had seldom been done before had happened: police officers had been found guilty and sentenced. It resulted in more civil police behavior toward street children in Belo Horizonte. Our teams were also treated with more respect. The number of street children killed in other Brazilian cities was regrettably still on the rise, but in Belo Horizonte there was a steep decline.

This tragedy also resulted in a more intense cooperation with local churches. Several pastors and members of their congregations ventured out at night to minister to street children. Others cooked and distributed large pots of soup. Churches opened their doors during the week to street children for day care or began halfway houses. God had used the whole episode for good.

TWENTY-FIVE

Changing Gears

T H E ministry was growing to a new level as more and more staff joined the various outreaches, and new outreaches were begun. At the same time my health forced me to delegate many responsibilities. For weeks I had had severe stomach pains and finally decided to see a doctor.

"You have an ulcer, ma'am," the doctor announced as he eyed me over the rim of his spectacles. "You'll have to slow down."

An ulcer? Wasn't I much too young to have an ulcer?

We decided to take a vacation and rework our schedules. It was obvious we had physical limitations. How could the ministry continue to grow without our constant supervision? The only solution was to delegate more tasks to other qualified people. The Lord had blessed us with many excellent and capable coworkers who were already carrying substantial responsibilities.

Jan and Sofia were two such coworkers.

"We would like to see a team work with the children in the slums," we had told Jan and Sofia. "It would be a preventive program so that the children of the slums won't leave for the streets." Since most of the street children came from the slums, it made sense to not only help those who were already on the streets but also try to keep children from ending up on the streets. We had often shared the gospel and played our puppet shows in those slums. We were grateful when Jan and Sofia agreed to take a team to work in those areas. Filled with enthusiasm, they started out. Pretty soon they had children's clubs meeting in classrooms of local churches where they kept the children happy all afternoon with Bible stories, songs, and crafts.

Jan and Sofia wanted to expand and began looking for a home in the slums where they and the other team members could live and be in more direct contact with these people.

"I think we've found a good house to buy," Jan announced one day. After some prayer they bought it. But after paying the agreed-upon price, another man appeared claiming to be the rightful owner and insisting upon compensation. Since the price of the house had been very low, Jan paid him as well. But then a third "owner" showed up. Jan decided that was the end of acquiring that house, even though it meant losing several hundred dollars. After searching more weeks for a house that would serve their needs, Jan finally found the ideal house. This one was built on a hill and from one side had a wide view of the whole city. The other side overlooked a slum with at least sixty thousand people.

This home did have legitimate owners, who seven years earlier had started to build what they had hoped would one day be a large mansion. However, during the extended building period they acquired new neighbors who discovered the open terrain adjacent to their property. Within a few years the land had become a sprawling mass of squatters amidst dusty dirt roads, plastic cubicle homes, and a few dilapidated concrete structures. The value of the property took a nosedive. In addition, the owners didn't feel safe anymore and needed armed guards to protect their property against intruders from the slums. Eventually they decided to sell the house and offered it to us at way below market value. I wondered whether God had intended this home for us seven years ago, since it was just perfect for our purpose.

I realized that little by little the devil was losing his foothold on death, violence, and sin in the slums. We were taking it for the Lord! Of course, there was a battle. This time our van wasn't stolen, but the Sunday before the final papers were signed, with Jan behind the wheel and ten coworkers inside, it skidded off the road and rolled over several times. A crowd of onlookers quickly gathered. Frightened but unhurt, Jan was able to get out of the van. Inside was a mix of arms and legs and bodies. Miraculously, everyone managed to get out unharmed and, on shaky legs, gathered around the van. They all had a few scratches and scrapes but no broken bones or serious injuries. They had been supernaturally protected!

"Hi, folks!" Jan addressed the crowd drawn by the accident. "Do you know who steals our joy?" He was referring to the theme of one of our puppet stories. "Do you know who is the thief? Well, there is someone who is much more powerful than that thief. If you hang in there for a moment, we'll show you!"

Shaken but with a grateful heart, our team pulled the puppets out of the wrecked van and presented the puppet show. That same week we bought the house on the hill and called it the Lighthouse.

"I BELIEVE this is the time to get a home for children with AIDS," Carla announced one day. For two years she had been visiting a small hospital on the edge of town. It was the only place in our vast city that admitted children with AIDS, and their numbers were increasing rapidly.

Denival, a fourteen-year-old street kid, was the first patient she visited. He was emaciated and deathly ill. No one visited him. For a month our staff ministered to him. They played board games and read Bible stories. His eyes lit up every time they arrived and sat next to his bed. Gladly, he prayed to receive the Lord. He knew he was a child of God. He had never known his earthly father, but now he had a heavenly Father. He had never known love or compassion, but now he was surrounded by it. He died in peace.

The deathly illness spread like wildfire. Street children were often abused by adult male homosexuals in exchange for a meal or some change. They themselves were also sexually promiscuous. Belo Horizonte's health care system was not prepared for this influx. There were only fifteen beds in this one small hospital, and most of them were occupied by adults and not by street children without families. We had heard about one boy who had been driven from one hospital to another for four days. Even though the boy was critically ill, no one wanted to admit him. The fourth day he died in the car. There had been no room for him.

We found a magnificent home for sale. It had four stories, sixteen large rooms, spacious bathrooms, several kitchens, and a huge garden with a variety of fruit trees. Johan, Carla, and I decided to pray about it.

Lord, is this the home You have in mind for the children with AIDS?

We had a hard time believing this ourselves. It was such an incredibly beautiful property. Wouldn't it be too luxurious? We took our time to be still before the Lord and allow Him to speak to us.

After a few minutes, Carla was the first to speak up. "I believe God is saying that He doesn't want children with AIDS in a house of death and sadness but wants them in a home of joy and life. With all those blossoming fruit trees, it really gives the impression of abundant life."

"Yes," Johan agreed, "it's as though God is saying He wants to give those sick children with AIDS an abundance of beauty."

My heart was warmed, for I, too, felt that God had spoken to me along these lines. *Those kids with AIDS, rejected by society as scum, are of great value to Me. This home is not too good for them. I want to bless them. I want to give them, through the loving care you provide, My love, warmth, joy, and security during those last few weeks, months, or years they have left on earth.*

Tears filled Carla's eyes. This was the reason God had called her to Brazil.

The Dutch Christian television management let us know by fax that they agreed with our plans and would make another substantial gift available. We bought the home and called it Refuge House. Soon Carla had acquired a team of dedicated workers.

One of the neighbors of Refuge House panicked when he found out we were going to admit children with AIDS. Afraid that the street would be littered with dying children and hence would devaluate his property, he tried to warn the entire neighborhood. He went door to door, distributed fliers, hung posters, and called the newspapers, television, and radio. His scare tactics alluded to the erroneous "fact" that

AIDS could be spread by mosquitoes or just by air currents and thus the whole neighborhood could get infected.

His actions had remarkable results but not the kind he had lobbied for. The entire neighborhood got involved all right—by solidly standing behind us! Neighbors took up collections, children dropped off toys, and young people volunteered their time to help. The home didn't just get local attention; it became national news. Christians everywhere became motivated, and churches got involved. As a result we developed specialized training to care for children with AIDS—the HIV/AIDS school. This brought even more people to Refuge House. God used this man's opposition to further His work. No neighbor could stop Him. Children were lovingly cared for at Refuge House while dozens of other children and their families were ministered to at their own homes.

Sometimes when I needed a quiet place to write newsletters or take care of other paperwork, I used one of the rooms at Refuge House. One day I had fled the phone and people at our own home and enjoyed the quiet serenity of this home. A five-year-old little girl with advanced AIDS was walking through the garden. When she came closer to my open window I could hear her singing a song that she made up as she walked along. She was totally absorbed in the song and unaware that I could hear her.

"Dear Lord Jesus, I am so happy. I love You. I'm going to live with You. You love me. Lord Jesus, I am coming. It's going to be beautiful to be with You."

I felt a lump in my throat.

Thank You, Lord, for Carla, for this home, for our staff. It's a privilege to be working for You and to see the transformation in these happy children.

Epilogue

AS THE ministry expanded, things didn't always go smoothly, but God used even opposition to further His plans to reach the people of Brazil and beyond. From new works in Brazil to new ministries on other continents, God's love and power were evident in each outreach He brought to fruition and in each life He restored.

KING'S KIDS

God's blessing was unmistakable at the King's Kids summer camps we held during school vacation. Our humble start of one or two camps a year had expanded to twenty-two, each with about fifty kids, teenagers, and adults. Through the media of dance and song the campers proclaimed the message of peace with God in cities through-out Brazil. Many times our own family participated as well. Sometimes it got a little scary. I recall one time when we were on our way with a whole bunch of King's Kids to a maximum-security prison, where we had been given permission for the Kids to perform. The children were unusually quiet. For most of them it would be a first to see the inside of a prison. God used the children in a mighty way. The hardened prison-ers were moved to tears when they heard the Kids' simple stories about God's love. Twenty-seven of them knelt on the cold cement floor to give their hearts to Jesus. By that time the children had set aside their fears and were rejoicing in God's mighty work. The other teams came back with similar stories. These were exciting vacations for our entire family.

RESTORATION HOUSE AND RECANTO HOUSE

In the meantime, Rescue House continued its outreaches. Every day teams covered the city to find new homeless children and get them off the streets as soon as possible. Boys who, after a few weeks at Rescue

House, could not return to their own homes moved to Restoration House, while girls went to Recanto House.

Paulo married Ieda, a short, energetic Brazilian coworker. Before their marriage they had often discussed Paulo's two children. Paulo's mother was not able to keep them, and the children's biological mother wanted Paulo to have them. Eventually, Paulo and Ieda decided to add both children to their own family. It was wonderful to see Paulo's growing sense of responsibility, not just in his work but also in his personal life. Paulo is now overseeing all three homes, and everything is running smoothly. Restoration House is home to twenty-four boys off the streets, and twelve to seventeen girls stay at Recanto House.

FARM FOR THE HOMELESS

The work continued to grow. Eduardo, who had overseen the lengthy renovations at Rescue House, now had a team working with homeless men and wanted to expand his ministry. A farmhouse was for sale in Ouro Fino, in the south of our state. Ideally located at the bottom of a hill, it had a well, a lake, an orchard, a coffee plantation, and numerous cornfields. It would be a great place to minister to those homeless men.

Unlike street children, who are largely from city slums, most homeless adults come from rural areas, lured to the city in search of work. Once there, most of them are robbed of all their valuables. Without ID or cash, they can't even apply for a job. A farm, where they could kick their alcohol and other drug habits and learn a trade, would be an ideal environment for them.

Eduardo had recently become engaged to Sandra, a sweet, quiet, and hardworking coworker. The couple were dreaming of taking in as many homeless men as possible and showing them the love of God in word and deed. When we sought the Lord in prayer about this farm, He confirmed in our hearts that He wanted us to have this property. At first, we were a little uneasy—everything was happening so fast, and we had already bought a number of homes. However, God provided the funds for all of them, and they are all paid in full.

A few months later we celebrated the marriage of Eduardo and Sandra with some coworkers at the new farmhouse! Since then a steady stream of homeless men have moved to the farm, and many have met the Lord Jesus as their Savior.

MINISTRY TO THE DEAF

Partly because of our own disabled children, some coworkers wanted to set up an evangelism outreach specifically to the deaf. We even prepared deaf missionaries who, in turn, reached other deaf people with the gospel. Dilma loved the attention, as these workers practiced their signing on her. We got to know more and more deaf children, and before long we had found an ideal home for them as well. Deaf children are helped with their schoolwork, deaf teenagers can take computer classes, and the home has become a meeting place for the deaf where they can always hear about God's love.

SCHOOL FOR THE DISABLED

We also opened a small school for disabled children. Dilma and Davi were two of the first pupils. We had tried sending Davi to a regular school, but he was too far behind. We even wondered whether he would ever learn to read and write. Close to our home was a school for mentally disabled children that was willing to take him, but we realized after a few months that he wasn't being encouraged enough to learn. The teachers didn't even try to teach the children anything; they were just baby-sitters. Since that was not what we had in mind, we decided to open our own school. We began with the autistic son of a coworker and a paralyzed girl from Recanto House and our own two children. Much to our surprise, the children all made immediate progress. Davi even became interested in letters and words and, with great big scratchy letters, began to write. The loving, patient teacher was worth her weight in gold.

AMAZON MISSION

Jorge, the ex-street kid who now lived and worked in the Amazon jungles to evangelize unreached Indian tribes, was doing well. He even married another YWAM missionary, and the couple has two beautiful daughters.

FIRSTFRUITS

Our first ex-street children continued to do well. Many had graduated from the Restoration House training. Three were baptized and later were trained as car mechanics. Vitor even attended a Discipleship Training School. These children were our firstfruits of the ministry.

NATIONAL AND INTERNATIONAL GROWTH

The work expanded to other cities and even to other countries. God was now sending us a stream of workers. Soon we had over one hundred in our various Belo Horizonte ministries. As a result, YWAM ministries to street children expanded to ten other Brazilian cities.

Mati and his wife, Julie, moved to Recife in northeast Brazil. Recife, along with Rio de Janeiro, has the highest toll of street children murders. Mati and Julie acquired a small house in downtown Recife and later obtained a beautiful piece of property with several small houses on a hill overlooking the city. They also started a Rescue and Restore course, which Johan often went to teach. Mati and his team brought new hope to the street children of Recife.

The Rescue and Restore School is now taught regularly in other cities and countries as well. Street children are not just a Brazilian problem. In countries around the world where the rural population moves to the cities, children become homeless and end up sleeping in the streets.

Johan was invited to teach in Mozambique and Angola. He was there for several weeks and was deeply touched by the tremendous needs of children in these countries. After several weeks of praying and planning, Wanderley and Rosaria—two great staff workers—and their two daughters moved to Mozambique.

India was also on Johan's list. He visited five cities, where he spoke at conferences, preached, and taught about street children ministries. During one summer vacation our entire family went to India, having been invited to teach the Rescue and Restore School. A wonderful group of twenty-two students was waiting for us. We enjoyed this new experience, and it was a blessing to have our whole family involved in teaching the course. Our children had a good time, and it was a joy for Johan and me to teach. We also accompanied the students on several street mission trips in the city of Pune, where the training was being held.

Needs among street children in Pune were even greater than I had envisioned. I met girls who as children had been married to adult husbands and as soon as they began to menstruate, had to move in with these husbands. I spoke with an eleven-year-old who had been living with her forty-year-old husband for two years. She lived in a dump close to where we were teaching. She told me she had to keep her "home" clean and cook on dried cow pies that she had to search for early in the morning. She had to wash clothes at a small faucet, the only source of water for 150 families; she would stand in line waiting to use it beginning as early as 5:30 in the morning. If she did something wrong, she got a beating. My heart ached as I watched her looking at the puppets. She was still a child, but her childhood had been taken from her. How many children are living like she is in this vast country of over one billion people? How many street children are there?

At the end of the Rescue and Restore School, four groups of students left to work full-time with street and slum children in various other Indian cities. We praised God for their compassion. Since then we have received much positive feedback from India. At train stations, in slums, in hospitals, and at all kinds of other locations, teams are reaching out to children who exist in the most deprived of circumstances. The Lord is blessing their work!

Ministries for children with AIDS have also expanded to several countries in Africa, South America, and Europe. Johan and some of our long-term staff are often invited to teach about children at risk in many different countries.

We thank the Lord for the many coworkers who reach out to children in need all over the world, and we pray that many children will get to know His great love for them.

Ministries and Homes of YWAM, Rescue and Restore, in Belo Horizonte, Brazil

1. RESCUE HOUSE

The team from Rescue House makes first contact with the children on the streets, seeking their recuperation and reintegration into society.

2. RESTORATION HOUSE

Street boys from broken homes go through a triage and then the various phases of the Restoration House program until they are ready to be completely reintegrated into society.

3. RECANTO HOUSE

Street girls come to Recanto House, where they go through a process of restoration and healing until they are ready to be completely reintegrated into society.

4. REFUGE HOUSE

Abandoned children who have HIV/AIDS are taken to Refuge House, where they are cared for in a family environment and come to know the love and acceptance of Father God.

5. THE LIGHTHOUSE

The team from the Lighthouse helps to meet the needs of the residents of one of the largest slums in Belo Horizonte.

6. "LET THEM HEAR!" HOUSE OF THE SOWER

The team of "Let Them Hear!" shows the love of God to deaf children, teenagers, and young adults and offers help with their needs in society, education, and family relationships.

7. RENEW HOUSE

A small orphanage for children without families. The goal is to find Brazilian Christian adoptive parents for them.

8. PROJECT BELIEVE

The missionaries of Project Believe bring the adult street people to a knowledge of God and to recuperation and reintegration in society.

9. PROJECT MANASSE

Project Manasse is dedicated to helping people who struggle with homosexual practices or desires.

10. EVANGELISM

The team of evangelism presents Jesus Christ as the only hope for salvation and fulfillment through dance, mime, personal evangelism, etc.

11. DISCIPLESHIP TRAINING SCHOOL

DTS is a six-month course focusing on the basics of the Christian walk and providing a short-term missionary experience. It is a prerequisite to becoming a full-time missionary with YWAM.

12. RESCUE AND RESTORE SCHOOL

In the Rescue and Restore School, given in Portuguese and English, students learn to reach and help children and adolescents on the streets and evangelize and minister in community centers in slums.

13. HIV/AIDS SCHOOL

The HIV/AIDS (**H**IV **I**ntervention **V**ia **A**ssistance, **I**ntercession, **D**iscipleship, and **S**alvation) School (taught in Portuguese and English) teaches students how to work among children, adolescents, and adults with HIV/AIDS.

MULTIPLICATION

The YWAM Rescue and Restore Ministries seek to provide a model of care given to street children and homeless adolescents, families struggling to survive in the slums, and people infected with HIV.

Through the Rescue and Restore School and the HIV/AIDS School, offered by the base in Belo Horizonte, many missionaries are being trained to establish works similar to those being done by Rescue, Restoration, Recanto, Refuge, and Renew Houses, House of the Sower, and the Lighthouse, in Brazil and in developing countries, mainly in India and on the continent of Africa.

How You Can Help

T H E following are five options for those who would like to participate in our ministries:

1. Become a full-time staff worker by (a) successfully completing a Discipleship Training School (DTS) and (b) making an initial commitment of two years.
2. Volunteer for one to three months.
3. Help the ministry through donations of useful items or financial gifts.
4. Financially support a YWAM missionary.
5. Pray for this work and the people involved.

Tax deductible gifts for the ministry in Belo Horizonte can be sent to

YWAM
P.O. Box 3000
Garden Valley, TX 75771
USA

Checks should be made payble in U.S. dollars to YWAM. Please include a separate note explaining that the gift is for Rescue and Restore Urban Ministries, Belo Horizonte, Brazil.

Johan and Jeannette Lukasse can be reached at
YWAM Rescue and Restore Urban Ministries
Caixa Postal 438
30123-970 Belo Horizonte, MG
Brazil
South America
Phone: 0055-31-3444-0912
Fax: 0055-31-3442-7567
E-Mail: jeannette@jocum.org.br
Website: www.jocum.org.br/bhcentro

What Leaders Are Saying about the YWAM Ministry in Belo Horizonte

"YWAM Belo Horizonte's urban ministry has influenced me personally. I believe it is a blessing not just to Belo Horizonte but to all the nations."

—*Armando Benner, YWAM Base Director, Amsterdam*

"Johan and Jeannette have been a great encouragement to us in South Asia in their sacrificial commitment to coming here to Pune and running the Rescue and Restore school. This school has resulted in lasting fruit of new ministries starting in three locations in India."

—*Steve Cochrane, YWAM Director of South Africa*

"It has been my privilege to see with my own eyes and hold one of the handicapped street children who has been provided a home, nurture, and spiritual well-being as the fruit of the urban ministry in Belo Horizonte. I highly recommend this ministry; I believe it is a model for many of the urban centers of the world."

—*Don Stephens, President & CEO, Mercy Ships International*

"Few ministries surpass YWAM Belo Horizonte in expressing God's tender love to the world's outcasts. I fully endorse this work and encourage all members of the body of Christ to give their support."

—*D. Leland Paris, YWAM Director of the Americas*

"Youth With A Mission is one of the few international mission organizations that give the subject of caring for the poor and needy more than just the odd module or course subject here and there. The street children challenge is one of the most relevant challenges facing the body of Christ today. I highly commend this ministry of YWAM Belo Horizonte."

—*Brother Daniel, International Coordinator: AD2000 (CPNRN)*

"As I walked the streets and saw the desperate needs, I have been deeply impacted by the work of YWAM's urban street ministry in Belo Horizonte, Brazil."

—Floyd McClung, Director YWAM Trinidad, Colorado, USA

"Since Johan and Jeannette started the work with the needy, our team in Belo Horizonte has been an example of the true love of God. I feel privileged and honored to call them my brothers and sisters, my coworkers."

—Jim Stier, Former International President of YWAM

"Throughout history the gospel has had its greatest power when the proclamation of God's love is combined with its demonstration. The YWAM urban ministry in Belo Horizonte is one of the clearest models of that combination I have seen in thirty years of ministry."

—Bob Moffitt, Ph.D., President, Harvest Foundation

"We have been very grateful for the Dutch connection with the street children ministry in Belo Horizonte over the years. We commend Johan and Jeannette and their team for this significant work of the Kingdom."

—Jeff Fountain, Regional Director, YWAM Europe

(left)
*Johan and
Jeannette on their
wedding day*
(below)
*Johan, Jeannette,
and Pieter*

(right)
*Jeannette (holding
baby Michele),
Johanneke, Johan,
and Pieter*

(above)
Johan, Jeannette,
and Pieter in front
of the Anastasis
(left)
The "miracle fish"
on the beach in
Greece

(above)
Kalafi Moala
praying for Dilma
(right)
Three-and-a-half-
year-old Dilma

Johanneke, Johan, Dilma, Jeannette, Michele, and Pieter

Michele, Johanneke, Dilma, Pieter, Jeannette, and Johan

(right and below)
Davi, just after he
was adopted at
age four

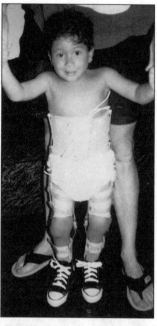

(counterclockwise) Jeannette, Pieter, Johanneke, Davi, Michele, Dilma, and Johan

Pieter, Michele, Johanneke, Davi, and Dilma

Sonia, the first street girl, with Dilma and Michele

(above)
Johan with one of
the first groups of
street kids in 1987
(right)
A girl living on
the streets

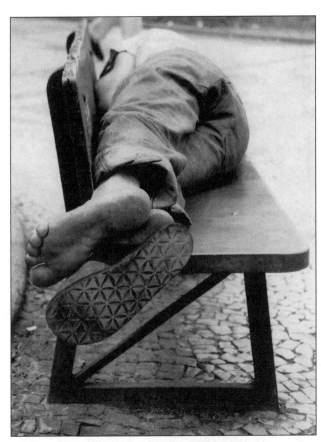

(left)
The feet of a
street child
(below)
Johan praying
with street kids

(right)
A lonely street child
(below)
Mati praying for
breakfast with the
street children

(above)
Carla taking the first child with AIDS into the Refuge House
(left)
Johan building the Restoration House

A gang of street kids

Boys living on the street

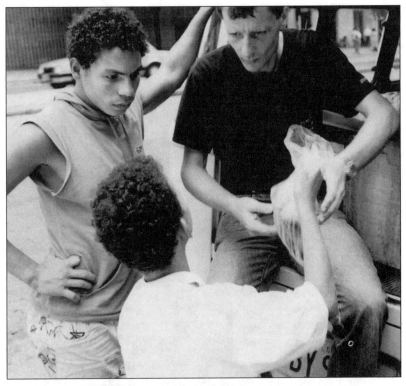

Johan and Jorge, a former street kid who later became a missionary among Indians in the Amazon region, handing out food on the streets

Street boys

(above)
Students of the
Rescue and Restore
School receiving
their diplomas
(right)
Johanneke, Michele,
Dilma, Johan, Jeannette,
Pieter, and Davi

Author Jeannette Lukasse

Christian Heroes: Then & Now

Adventure-filled Christian biographies for ages 10 to 100!

Readers of all ages love the exciting, challenging, and deeply touching true stories of ordinary men and women whose trust in God accomplished extraordinary exploits for His kingdom and glory.

Gladys Aylward: The Adventure of a Lifetime • 1-57658-019-9
Nate Saint: On a Wing and a Prayer • 1-57658-017-2
Hudson Taylor: Deep in the Heart of China • 1-57658-016-4
Amy Carmichael: Rescuer of Precious Gems • 1-57658-018-0
Eric Liddell: Something Greater Than Gold • 1-57658-137-3
Corrie ten Boom: Keeper of the Angels' Den • 1-57658-136-5
William Carey: Obliged to Go • 1-57658-147-0
George Müller: The Guardian of Bristol's Orphans • 1-57658-145-4
Jim Elliot: One Great Purpose • 1-57658-146-2
Mary Slessor: Forward into Calabar • 1-57658-148-9
David Livingstone: Africa's Trailblazer • 1-57658-153-5
Betty Greene: Wings to Serve • 1-57658-152-7
Adoniram Judson: Bound for Burma • 1-57658-161-6
Cameron Townsend: Good News in Every Language • 1-57658-164-0
Jonathan Goforth: An Open Door in China • 1-57658-174-8
Lottie Moon: Giving Her All for China • 1-57658-188-8
John Williams: Messenger of Peace • 1-57658-256-6
William Booth: Soup, Soap, and Salvation • 1-57658-258-2
Loren Cunningham: Into All the World • 1-57658-199-3

Available from YWAM Publishing
1-800-922-2143
www.ywampublishing.com

Also available: Christian Heroes Unit Study Curriculum Guides